if you 're

clueless

about

saving

money

and

want to

know more

by SETH GODIN

Dearborn
Financial Publishing, Inc.®

If You're Clueless about Saving Money and Want to Know More

Executive Editor: Cynthia A. Zigmund
Managing Editor: Jack Kiburz
Interior and Cover Design: Karen Engelmann

© 1997 by Seth Godin Productions, Inc.

Published by Dearborn Financial Publishing, Inc.®

Printed in the United States of America

97 98 99 10 9 8 7 6 5 4 3 2

Library of Congress Cataloging-in-Publication Data
Godin, Seth.
    If you're clueless about saving money and want to know more / by Seth Godin.
       p.   cm.
    Includes index.
    ISBN 0-7931-2556-1 (paper)
    1. Finance. Personal--United States.   2. Investments--United States.   I. Title.
  HG179.G636   1997
  332.024--dc21   97-5609
                                                               CIP

Acknowledgments

Thanks to Jack Kiburz and Cindy Zigmund at Dearborn whose editorial guidance made this book possible. Karen Watts was the driving force behind the Clueless concept, and Pamela Rohland and Susan Kushnick did an expert job of pulling it all together.

Thanks to Robin Dellabough, Lisa DiMona, Nana Sledzieski, Leslie Sharpe, Lisa Lindsay, Julie Maner, and Sarah Silbert at SGP for their never-ending insight and hard work. And kudos to Sidney Short for his layout work, Betsy Beacom and Gwen Bronson for their copyediting talent, and Suzanne Herel for her proofreading skills.

Contents

GETTING *a clue* about *saving* MONEY

Do you want to live comfortably and know that your future is **financially secure?** Do you want to have the kind of financial **freedom** that empowers you to make your own choices and run your own show, no matter how long you live?

No matter where you find yourself right now, financial independence is within your reach. All it requires is rethinking the ways you spend your money. By planning, organizing, and setting some priorities, you can make a commitment to saving money. The reward is a life of comfort that lets you do the things you want to do, buy the things you want to buy, and relax on a cushion of money that you've created yourself.

Traditional methods of saving money bring to mind visions of forfeiting today's creature comforts for the pleasures of tomorrow. But that's not what this book is all about.

It's not about denial and sacrifice. It's about giving up little things that don't mean much to you, to save for the things that will make you happy. It's about formulating good spending and saving habits that will last you a lifetime.

Write Your Own Financial Declaration of Independence

If you follow the guidelines in this book, you'll be able to save enough to free yourself from anxiety about money. And once you've done that, you can channel that energy in positive directions to do the things you've dreamed of doing and pave the way to grow emotionally, spiritually, and intellectually without financial worries.

You need to think about money as a tool—nothing more, nothing less—that you use to get what you want out of life. Since this book is as much about spending money as it is about saving it, you'll learn how to use this tool to get the things you want.

Take Some Pictures of Yourself

So what do you want out of life? How do you figure out what's really important to you? You do this by taking two pictures of yourself. The first picture will help you determine your net worth. It's a very black-and-white profile of exactly how much you have financially—your assets (how much you own) and your liabilities (how much you owe).

The other picture, your spending profile, is more colorful. By answering a series of questions, you'll be able to define your lifestyle by seeing just where your money goes. And you'll be able to determine just what you can give up easily to get what you want.

In chapter two, we'll help you take the first of these snapshots. But you need to retake these pictures on a regular basis—once a year on your

STRING SAVER #1

Keep a bottle of drinking water in the refrigerator rather than running the faucet to cool the water.

How Much Money Do You Need to Save?

This table shows minimum total savings needed by couples and individuals at various income and age levels to remain on track for a comfortable retirement. Because women typically work fewer years than men and earn less, they need more savings.

Recommended Savings by Age

Household Characteristics:	35	45	55	65
Married Couples Earning $35,000				
With pension	$ 570	$ 15,110	$ 52,250	$ 88,470
Without pension	5,100	35,420	82,830	138,100
Earning $110,000				
With pension	37,120	119,400	287,810	530,000
Without pension	62,250	186,200	403,250	690,350
Single Men Earning $35,000				
With pension	3,170	27,380	65,990	95,980
Without pension	11,350	49,520	103,250	150,650
Earning $45,000				
With pension	6,130	34,110	94,700	171,210
Without pension	23,300	82,900	173,920	280,360
Single Women Earning $35,000				
With pension	25,000	49,540	81,660	107,670
Without pension	35,180	71,200	114,360	155,600
Earning $45,000				
With pension	34,650	72,850	126,800	189,960
Without pension	54,710	115,820	194,620	285,000

birthday works well—because the patterns will change as you grow. And as things change, your needs and wants will change, too.

A Kinder, Gentler Savings Plan

If setting up a savings plan seems totally overwhelming to you, take heart. This is a kind and gentle plan that eases you into a new way of thinking about money. It's not designed to torture you or deprive you of the things you enjoy. If you follow these simple steps, you'll be that much closer to achieving the financial security that will enable you to get exactly what you want now and later.

1. Identify your short-, medium-, and long-term goals.

2. Determine which of these goals are most important to you.

3. Reduce debt.

4. Set up your savings plan choosing from the options you'll learn about in this book.

5. Increase your income. That doesn't necessarily mean that you have to run out and get a job that pays a lot more money or moonlight on weekends. Financial security doesn't depend on how much you earn. It depends on how much you manage to save. And the beauty of this plan is that this last step will happen automatically if you follow the first four steps.

Financial Security Is Not Just for the Wealthy...and Not All Rich People Are Financially Secure

There are doctors and lawyers who earn six-figure incomes but have no long-term financial security because they have nothing saved; they spend every penny they make. And there are people who earn more modest amounts but have managed to keep cushions in reserve. In some cases, a secretary who is committed to financial planning may have more financial security than a surgeon.

There are also rich people who are totally preoccupied with their finances. (Maybe that's how they got all that money in the first place.) But a life that focuses exclusively on getting and keeping money is not exactly a well-rounded one. And obsessing about every cent you spend is unnecessarily stressful.

People with lots of money make decisions about spending priorities all the time. Do I want the Porsche or the Land Rover? Do I go skiing or to Puerto Rico for Christmas vacation? Italian restaurant or French tonight? Having enough money to do whatever you want doesn't eliminate the need to make choices.

Get Savvy about Savings

If you're between the ages of 21 and 45, tucking a portion of your paycheck away in a low-interest savings account will not combat the demons that threaten your nest egg: longer life expectancy, higher inflation, job insecurity, and the burden of funding retirement needs that's shifting from the employer to the employee.

This book will show you how to get wise about the big guns of saving—stocks, bonds, mutual funds, and tax-free retirement accounts—so the money you have earmarked for saving will grow and work for you.

You'll learn how to protect your investments and savings with a life insurance plan so that unpleasant surprises don't catch you with your pants down.

YOU CAN BE FINANCIALLY SECURE

Define Your Financial Goals: (Answers for each are: Immediate, Mid-range, Long-term, Not at all)

- Reducing debt

- Building a nest egg

- Buying a house

- Making home improvements

- Buying a car

- Providing for children's education

- Increasing insurance coverage

- Taking a vacation

- Living more comfortably

- Taking an unpaid leave from work

- Starting a business

- Retiring early

You'll receive a crash course on real estate and mortgages, and discover how to save money when you're buying the house of your dreams.

And you'll get the lowdown on retirement planning because, believe it or not, you need to start right now, in order to have enough socked away by the time you're ready to start winding down your career.

But perhaps most important of all, you'll see how your attitudes about spending money affect the way you save. You'll discover how to make choices you can live with and how to rearrange your thinking so you spend less, save more, and feel comfortable and secure knowing you are building a life of financial security.

Get Down to the Nitty-Gritty: What's Your Net Worth?

Before you can make realistic choices about how to spend and save your money, you need to figure out exactly how much you're worth. Think of yourself as a business and work up a detailed financial plan, because once you see how much is coming in and going out on a monthly basis, you'll be able to determine how much you have left over to save and invest. Use this worksheet to calculate your assets (what you have) and your liabilities (what you pay out). It might take you a few hours to do this right. Dig out last month's bank statement and your checkbook register and add up the real numbers. Don't just guess.

Net Asset Worksheet

Current Assets

    Checking account balance   *0*

    Savings account balance   *0*

    Investment portfolio (stocks, bonds, mutual funds, CDs, and so on)   *12,000*

    Real estate   *25,000*

    Life insurance   *0*

    Personal property (car, furniture, clothing, valuables)   *15,000*

Monthly Receivables

    Salary

    Dividends from investments

    Interest from savings accounts

    Income from trust funds or family income

    Self-employed income

Liabilities

    Housing (rent, mortgage, maintenance)

    Utilities

    Insurance premiums

    Medical

    Groceries

    Clothing expenses

    Entertainment

    Transportation

Debt

    Credit card balances

    Loans

Now that you've filled in this worksheet, go back and take a good hard look at the numbers. Ask yourself some of the same questions any business owner has to ask when assessing the financial health of his or her company. What is my cash flow situation like? Am I taking in more money than is going out every month? If so, where is that extra money going and what can I modify in my spending to create a surplus? Do I have any money saved for a rainy day? If not, what can I do to begin building that stash?

Your Spending Profile

You can't figure out how to cut back your expenses until you know exactly where your money is going. Then you can carve out a portion of your income to stash in a savings plan. Now that you've got a picture of your net worth, it's time to take a picture of your spending profile. This is easy. Think about the things you like to do. Get out your checkbook, credit card statements and a list of cash withdrawals from the ATM and make a list of your expenses for the past three months. Trace your steps to find out where the money was spent. Put your expenses into the following categories: shelter (include furnishings, home improvements, and repairs), food, clothes, transportation (include commuting costs and all your car expenses), utilities, entertainment/recreation (include vacations), medical care, insurance, miscellaneous. (This is really a very personalized list and you may need to add categories that are specific only to you.) See where the majority of your money goes. What's the biggest expense?

Now put these categories in order of importance to you. Is where you live high on the priority list? What about your set of wheels? Is it basic transportation or does it need to say more? Do you like to take vacations? Are you committed to exercise and fitness? After you've ordered your priorities, see what made it to the top and what fell to the bottom. That bottom is the key. This is where you need to trim the fat. It won't hurt—you just decided it's not that important, anyway. Decide how many categories you want to eliminate. But remember, the more expenses you cut, the more money you can save. And the more you save, the closer you'll be to financial freedom.

Set Goals

Now it's time to identify your short-term goals (less than two years), your mid-range goals (three to nine years) and your long-term goals (ten years or more). Some typical goals are buying a house or car, saving for children's college education, starting a business, taking a major trip, and retiring early. While you're thinking about this, don't forget to put buying adequate insurance policies high on the list. It may sound dull and unimportant, but a lack of insurance can jeopardize savings and financial security if disaster strikes.

Set a timetable to achieve each of your goals, but be realistic. Focus on what you believe is attainable, taking into account the lifestyle you and the rest of your family want to lead. Planning to lead the life of a miser in order to meet financial goals will only doom you to failure. Be honest about what you can do.

Keep Good Records

When the plan is in place, keep good records. The easiest way to do this is to hold on to cash receipts, checkbook entries, and credit card statements. (If you've been recording these electronically, you may want to have a handwritten record of these to use as backup, in case something happens to your computer files.)

Review the records regularly to find out where your financial "leaks" are. If you learn, for example, that unreimbursed entertainment expenses take up 25 percent of your paycheck, that signals a problem, and you can start to search for a solution.

Is a Financial Planner for You?

Some people choose to consult a financial planner to help them chart their future course and keep track of their progress. This is a personal decision. Some people don't want to take the time to learn about financial planning, so they turn to a professional. A good financial planner, like a good therapist, will walk with you through trouble areas, hold your hand, and help you find your own answers by providing sound information. You can work with a financial planner to help you:

- *Get advice on tax issues*. Instead of trying to save money by doing your own taxes or going to a tax preparer who does little more than prepare the paperwork, it pays to consult a professional to learn some specific ways to cut down on

STRING SAVER #2

Before making a purchase, take two separate shopping trips—the first to compare prices and quality, the second to buy. Avoid carrying credit cards, a checkbook, or much cash on the comparison shopping trip. After the second trip when you've made your actual purchase, calculate how much you've saved and reward yourself with a small present that costs 10 percent of the savings total. Invest the rest in your savings plan.

Fifteen Ways to Turn a Wasted Dollar into a Saved Dollar

You know you'd snatch a fallen dollar from the street in a microsecond. So why do you fritter away those that are already in your wallet?

To Waste a Dollar	To Save a Dollar
1. Buy a lottery ticket.	Put that $1 into a "lottery fund." Tuck it into an envelope, piggy bank, or shoe box. When you have saved even $10, deposit it into an interest-bearing account.
2. Eat in restaurants.	Take the $25 you would have spent for dinner in a regular restaurant, or the $5 you would have spent at a burger joint for lunch, and create a "restaurant fund." When you have $100, open an interest-bearing savings account. Plan to convert that savings account to a higher interest mutual fund when you have amassed the minimum deposit required (and treat yourself to a celebratory dinner in a restaurant!).
3. Buy a new car every few years.	Take money you would have spent on a new car and invest it in a mutual fund.
4. Use high-interest gold cards.	If you must use a credit card, use American Express, which requires you to pay off the balance every month.
5. Buy designer clothing.	If you must have those designer labels, buy them on sale or at outlets. Or buy a few pieces of clothing that coordinate so you can mix and match.

To Waste a Dollar	To Save a Dollar
6. Buy trendy clothing.	Buy classics that can be worn season after season, and if you can't resist the trendy, indulge in accessories.
7. Keep your money in a savings account.	Invest in mutual funds and low-risk equities that give you greater returns than a savings account.
8. Give in to impulse shopping on cable television.	If you can't stop yourself, pull the plug on your cable. You'll save money on shopping expenses, and on the cable bill.
9. Buy something on sale that you don't need.	If you're not absolutely sure you need it, you probably don't. Wait one day and think over the purchase.
10. Buy full-priced merchandise.	Watch like a hawk for sales. Become familiar with the discount stores and outlets in your community.
11. Spend vested pension benefits.	Roll them over into an IRA when you leave your job.
12. Give lavish gifts.	Give homemade gifts like food and crafts. People will appreciate your thoughtfulness and will cherish the gifts more.
13. Buy property you've never seen.	Take the money you would have spent and invest it into your retirement fund.
14. Take investment tips from a stranger.	Do your research and rely on your own instincts.
15. Pay credit card interest and late charges.	Pay bills in full at the end of every month.

Financial Profiles: If You Are...

Starting to Fly (25 to 34 years old): Your career is just getting off the ground and you are starting to juggle a lot of new financial obligations: rent, car payments, student loan payments. Your paycheck is about $480 a week, and you don't have much to put aside. You probably have a checking or savings account, but you don't have a retirement plan.

You should start a regular savings program now, stashing away at least 10 percent of your salary. Now is also the best time for you to start planning for your golden years. If you put aside $2,000 a year in an Individual Retirement Account earning 8 percent, by the time you're 65, you'll have $315,000.

Building Momentum (35 to 44 years old): You're making some progress. Your paycheck is fatter—about $692 a week. Maybe you have a retirement account, but with the obligations of a mortgage and raising a family, you still don't have a lot left over to invest.

If you want to achieve some long-term financial security, cut your spending and debt as much as possible. If you're frittering away money or using credit cards heavily, stop. Every time you say no to yourself for something you don't really need, you have more money to spend on the things that matter to you.

Already There (45 to 54 years old): The hard work paid off. You're making more money than you ever have, about $826 a week. You have a retirement account and have established long-term investments.

Still, you're not in the clear. Your kids are going to college and your aging parents may need some financial assistance. But don't stop saving for your own future. Pay your savings account before you pay anything else.

your personal tax bill. According to Ernst & Young, a leading accounting firm, a good financial planner can show you how to anticipate your financial decisions with taxes in mind so you're making the right moves throughout the year rather than waiting until tax preparation time.

- *Save time on researching various investment vehicles*. There's lots of information out there about financial planning and investing—in magazines and books, and on the Internet. But if you're too busy to do the extensive research to be a well-informed investor, a financial planner will be able to provide you with a thumbnail sketch of stocks, mutual funds, bonds, Treasury securities, and other products, and will give you a bottom-line approach to determining which investments are best for you.

STRING SAVER #3

Unless it's an emergency, don't check into a hospital on a Friday. Most hospitals aren't fully staffed over the weekend, so you may wind up waiting until Monday to have tests and other procedures done—while the meter ticks all weekend. The best check-in day is Tuesday. The staff has caught up with the Monday rush and will be able to tend to your needs more efficiently.

There are two kinds of financial planners. Commission-based planners provide advice, then they sell you products, such as insurance or investment products, to meet your needs. They work at insurance companies, brokerage houses, and financial planning firms. Customers pay for their services through commissions on the products purchased. The advantage, to the customer, is that the planner can provide a one-stop shopping service. The disadvantage is that questions may be raised about the planner's objectivity. Is he pitching a product because it offers a high commission?

Fee-based planners usually work for accounting firms. They get paid for their advice but do not sell the products they recommend, and they do not receive commissions. Customers may have a greater sense that the financial planner is objective because there is no vested interest in selling one product over another. The disadvantage is that the customer must pay a fee for each meeting, whether she acts on the advice or not.

Financial planners aren't magicians or miracle workers, and you shouldn't expect a planner to suddenly turn around a dire financial situation. Before settling on a financial planner, do your homework, just as you would if you were selecting a doctor. Anyone can hang out a financial planner shingle, and quality varies widely. Ask friends, lawyers, tax preparers, or bankers for referrals. Find out whether the planner is accredited. That doesn't guarantee quality, but it's a starting point. There are three main types of certification:

- *Accredited Personal Financial Specialist (APFS)*. This is awarded by the American Institute of Certified Public Accountants and is held only by CPAs. They usually operate on a fee-only basis.

- *Certified Financial Planner (CFP)*. Awarded by the College for Financial Planning in Denver, Colorado, this certification is granted to people who have completed a study program, passed an examination, and fulfilled a work experience requirement.

- *Chartered Financial Consultant*. This is awarded by the American Society of Chartered Life Underwriters and Chartered Financial Consultants in Bryn Mawr, Pennsylvania. The certification is granted to people who have completed a ten-section course of study and passed two exams.

You should be concerned about your financial planner if:

- Your plan seems generic and not customized to your situation. A one-size-fits-all plan might serve as a starting point, but it probably will not provide enough detail or direction to help you meet your goals.

- All the recommendations involve buying products that the planner will make a high commission on. You may be buying investment instruments you don't really need. This type of planner is most interested in his bottom line—not yours.

- The planner is very new in the field. A rookie will not have the same depth of experience as someone who has been in the field for several years and may overlook options that would benefit you. By the same token, someone who has been in the field a very long time may not have kept up with new developments and new methods of investing. Choose a planner who walks the middle ground, in terms of experience.

How will you know if your plan is specific enough? The financial planner should spend one or two meetings simply getting to know you, your financial background, your goals, and your tolerance for investment risk. Some planners provide new clients with a self-quiz to help target key areas of financial planning. If you are married, the planner should focus on both you and your spouse's answers and suggest investment alternatives as a couple and as individuals.

Good financial planners always take time to explain not only what investments should be made, but why they should be made and why a particular vehicle is the best one for you. They also discuss how your plan could be changed over time to help you meet new financial situations, such as the birth of a child or a divorce.

The more specific the information you provide, the better the chance a financial plan will be customized to meet your exact needs. Some questions the financial planner should ask you in order to provide a detailed plan include:

STRING SAVER #4

For one month, record everything you spend for food, including restaurant meals, vending machines, delis, and convenience stores. That is your real food budget. Look for areas where you can trim back, but also remember that you're not perfect—budget for splurges.

- What are your short-term, mid-range, and long-term goals? If you don't know what they are, talking with the planner should help you define them. No investing can begin without drawing this road map first.

- How comfortable do you feel with investment risk? This gives the planner a sense of how aggressively you want to invest. Good planners will not push you beyond your personal comfort level.

- How much money do you have set aside for emergencies? Investing should not begin until you have at least six months' salary set aside as an emergency fund. A good financial planner will not advise young people without adequate emergency funds to tie up most of their money in retirement plans, for example, because there are hefty taxes and penalties for withdrawing the money before age 59 1/2.

- What retirement plans does your employer provide, or, if you are self-employed, have you established a retirement plan of your own? This information will help the planner provide sound advice on retirement planning and recommend additional ways to save.

- What is your tax bracket and do you have any special tax considerations? In the course of your discussion, a planner may discover that you are not taking all of the deductions to which you are entitled or that you are having too much money withheld from your paycheck for taxes. Knowing about your tax situation will allow the planner to make sure that you aren't paying the government too much while not investing enough for yourself.

- How familiar are you with stocks, bonds, mutual funds, and so on? Never invest in something you don't understand—even if a financial planner tells you to do so. Ethical financial planners with your best interests at heart will take the time to explain the pros and cons of various investment opportunities, not simply try to sell you on a financial product.

Even if you hire a qualified, responsible, experienced financial planner, it doesn't mean you can give up control of your money. You still must educate yourself, because you make the final decisons. The planner only drives where you tell him to go.

START
to build
the foundation
for
SECURITY

CHAPTER TWO

You only live once—and if you use this life wisely, you can **enrich** yourself spiritually and financially. But if you're expending a good portion of your energy worrying about money, it will sap creativity and leave no room for making things happen the way you want them to.

If you think like an architect, you'll be able to build a savings plan that will free you from the chains of financial worries, and liberate you to pursue the goals most important to you.

17

Sometimes Things Have to Fall Apart Before You Can Reshape a New Beginning

One of the worst-case financial scenarios for any-one is declaring bankruptcy. It can be a humiliating and traumatic experi-ence. And it means that you need to start building your financial founda-tion from ground zero. But that doesn't mean it can't be done or that peo-ple who have declared bankruptcy cannot ever become financially secure. If it worked for Walt Disney, it can work for you. Experience is an excel-lent teacher. If the worst should happen to you, learn from it, and rebuild your financial plan using the lessons bankruptcy has taught you.

If debt problems become so severe that you start thinking about the "B" word, remember that declaring bankruptcy is an option of last resort and should not be considered lightly. It will eliminate some current debts, including credit card debt, medical and utility bills, auto loans, and rent. But it will not absolve you from paying alimony, child support, student loans, taxes, or court-ordered damages. And it ruins your credit rating for up to ten years. Think hard before you go this route, and ask for profes-sional advice.

The National Foundation for Consumer Credit has counselors who can help with money management, as well as offer advice and support. Look up their local chapters in your phone book and check the resources sec-tion on page 195 for their hotline.

A warning here, though. Avoid turning to places listed as "credit repair" clinics or "credit doctors." Some of them are for-profit scams that will only get you deeper in debt. They may promise results and have money-back guarantees, but you may find there are hidden strings or that the company has vanished when you want your money refunded. If you're ripped off by one of these places, call your state attorney general's office.

Step One: Set Goals

The first step is to set your sights on what you really want from life—now and in the near and distant future. A drop-dead wardrobe? A fancy car? Money to travel? Maybe a vacation bungalow or a nice home? A quality education for your children?

Step Two: Prioritize

The more experiences you have, the more you grow. And let's face it, most experiences, whether they're cultural, travel-related, recreational, or educational, cost money. If you don't have enough money to do everything you want, you need to prioritize. What do you want first? What can wait until later? Take that list of goals and put them in order.

Step Three: Demolish Debt

Tackling debt is the third step to building a solid financial foundation. Ignoring debt is like walking in quicksand—you're only going to sink in deeper.

- *Put the brakes on debt.* There are lots of reasons why otherwise intelligent people compromise their future with too much debt. A sudden illness or the loss of a job can wreak havoc with your financial plans. One of the biggest reasons people have too much debt is that they spend too much on impulse purchases. It's easy to succumb to small temptations: that cute sweater, that fancy thingamajig for the car. You don't have to be a shopaholic to run into trouble. The fact is that a string of small impulse buys can add up enough to derail your carefully laid financial plans. Uncontrollable impulse spending is a disorder, like compulsive gambling, that calls for professional help.

If you think you have a serious problem, contact a local Debtor's Anonymous program. The organization is founded to help people with debt or spending problems and is modeled after the 12-step Alcoholics Anonymous program. For more information, check your local phone book for the chapter near you.

Debt Counselors of America is a nonprofit organization designed to assist individuals and families with managing debt and financial difficulties. Some of its services are free, and it offers consultations by phone or by mail. See the resources section on page 195 for contact information.

- *Go on a spending diet.* A simple recipe for reducing debt quickly is to spend less. You can go cold-turkey by placing a moratorium on all unnecessary expenditures, or you can look at your priority list and drop some from the bottom. Areas that can often be trimmed include entertainment, travel, clothes, gifts, new cars, and expensive decorations for the home. If you can eliminate even one of those expenses, you can use the money to make a credit card payment.

STRING SAVER #5

Buy clothing at the end of the season. If you plan ahead, you can save megabucks on expensive items, such as sweaters and coats, by taking advantage of off-season sales. Be sure to store the items properly so they don't become damaged or moth-eaten.

- *Do something in your best interest.* Sometimes it makes sense to use your savings to pay off high-interest credit cards. If you're saving money and investing it at a rate of 7 percent interest but hanging on to a credit card bill that charges 17 percent, you're losing a lot of money. Pay off the credit card bill first, then invest.

This does more than remove a burden from your finances. It's like earning a windfall on your long-term investments. Think of it this way: If you pay off a credit card balance that racks up interest at 17 percent, getting rid of the debt is like earning 17 percent on an investment.

- *Double up.* If you can do it, make double payments on your credit card debt to remove it more quickly and cut the monthly service charges.

- *Consolidate debt.* Another way to reduce your burden is to consolidate debt or transfer it to another creditor who will charge a lower interest rate. You could get credit with a company offering a lower-rate credit card, then pay off the expensive debt with the cheaper debt. Or get a home equity loan. This allows borrowers to pay off high-rate credit cards with a lower-rate, tax-deductible loan at a substantial savings. But be aware of the risk. Home equity loans have very specific, rigid contractual terms. If you fall behind, you'll risk losing your home.

- *Repay your student loans.* Next to credit card debt, student loan debt is one of the major impediments to the financial health of younger people. Many of us know people who ignore student loan debt entirely, at great peril to their credit rating. But it doesn't have to be this way.

Programs exist through banks, credit unions, and the Student Loan Marketing Association to help graduates consolidate their federal student loans, allowing them to write only one repayment check per month. Contact them at (800) 643-0040.

The federal government also offers a direct loan consolidation program administered through the U.S. Department of Education. The consolidation allows students to extend repayment up to 30 years, if necessary, reducing monthly payments by up to 40 percent. Call (800) 557-7392 for more information.

To be eligible, you must have debt in one of the federal loan programs: Stafford, Health Professional Student, Perkins, Supplemental Loans for Students, and Parent Loans for Undergraduate Students. When the loans are consolidated, the interest rate for Stafford,

SEEK PROFESSIONAL FINANCIAL COUNSELING IF...

• You routinely go to more **expensive** stores or restaurants because they accept credit cards and you're short on cash.

• You've been asked to have a friend or relative co-sign a **loan.**

• Even though you've consolidated your debts into one lower-interest loan, **new bills** continue to come in, making an even larger debt.

• You **don't know** how much money you owe.

• If you lost your job, you **couldn't pay** next month's bills.

What to Do If You're In Too Deep

If you routinely spend more than you earn, choose one of the moonlighting businesses on page 29 to make up the difference.

If your monthly credit card and loan payments (excluding mortgage and car loans) exceed 20 percent of your pay after taxes, consolidate your debt with a lower-interest credit card or consolidation loan.

If this month's bills are piling up, and you haven't finished paying last month's and you're always making late payments and receiving notices about delinquent payments, consider getting a home equity loan to catch up.

If you have more than ten credit cards, including cards issued by gasoline companies and department stores, set priorities and decide which three you really need. Put the rest in a safe place and carry only the ones you've chosen.

If you're making only the minimum monthly payment on loans and the debt continues to rise, check your priorities to see if you're spending on things that are low on the list. Eliminate those expenses until you can catch up.

If you're taking cash advances on credit cards and using savings to pay basic monthly bills, such as rent, utilities, and food, or if you're using large credit lines to pay for current living expenses, you may want to consider moving to a less expensive home. Think of it as a lifestyle change and concentrate on the positive aspects of the move. Take the opportunity to improve the quality of your life rather than thinking of it as defeat. For example, if you're living in an apartment in a city, maybe it's time to think about the joys of suburban living—a little fresh air, some peace and quiet. You may even learn to enjoy it.

Perkins, and Supplemental Loans for Students are capped at 8.25 percent. The Parent Loans for Undergraduate Students are capped at 9 percent. Married couples can consolidate loans jointly.

Some lenders offer graduated repayments that start out lower during the first years out of school and gradually increase along with earnings as the former student establishes a career. Others offer an income-contingent plan, which lets your payment go up or down along with your income. This is a good option for people whose incomes may fluctuate quite a bit, such as the self-employed and salespeople.

While the program may be helpful, depending on your situation, be aware that sometimes the interest rate on the consolidated loan is higher than on the original loan, increasing the cost of borrowing. You don't want to be paying off the debt until you're 45 years old or older. It's a daunting prospect!

- *Make loan payments automatically from your checking account.* Some lenders are willing to give you a slight break on interest rates if loans are paid automatically. This is a fairly painless way to save cash, and it helps you stick with the repayment plan.

- *Borrow money only when you absolutely have to.* Borrowing should be an option of last resort and should be done only for absolute necessities.

KNOW WHERE YOU STAND

If you've been turned down for a loan or **denied credit,** find out why by obtaining a copy of your credit report, which is a history of your borrowing and payment. Sometimes mistakes appear on the report which damage your ability to obtain the funds you need.

To receive a copy of the report, contact a credit reporting agency and request it. The cost for the report is $2 to $15; if you've been denied credit within the past 30 days, the report is free.

If you see a mistake, contact the **credit agency** and the business which inaccurately reported the information.

To learn more about your rights under the **Fair Credit Reporting Act,** contact the Federal Trade Commission at (202) 326-2222.

Borrowing too quickly or too often is a good way to dig a deep hole for yourself that will take a long time to climb out of.

- *Use a debit card.* Debit cards work much like automatic teller machine cards. You have a set amount that you can spend and every purchase is subtracted from the total in your checking account. Although the debit card can't stop you from going on a shopping spree, it will bring a halt to spending when the till is empty. Knowing there is an absolute limit makes many people more conscious of their spending. It's like putting your need to go on a spending binge under a cold shower. Not all banks offer debit cards, though, so you may have to switch to one that does.

STRING SAVER #6

If you need to stay in a **hospital,** bring your own stuff—or as much as you possibly can. Hospitals charge an exorbitant amount for every little thing—every tissue you use, as well the pillows, linens, nightgowns, and slippers.

Before you check in, make a list of everything you could supply yourself, and bring it.

Step Four: Implement Your Savings Plan

Your savings plan will consist of several elements. They may range from a basic bank savings account to the slightly more complicated certificates of deposit, Treasury bills, and the most sophisticated investment instruments like stocks, bonds, and mutual funds. All of these will be covered a little later in this book.

How to Get Started

Start your savings plan simply by asking your employer to deduct a specific amount from your paycheck every week and deposit it in a savings account before you get your hands on it. By siphoning funds into your savings stash automatically, you'll never miss a payment, and you'll never be tempted to spend the cash. You've said "yes" to your dreams, you've got a nest egg at the ready, and you've bought yourself some peace of mind. It's the most painless route to saving. As you begin to become familiar

with the pros and cons of the various savings and investment routes discussed throughout this book, you can augment your plan with them.

Here are some other strategies for getting started:

- *Beef up your savings.* If your savings account is weak and puny, bulk it up with regular savings. You can do it. Your mother was right: A little here, a little there, and it all adds up. Ben Franklin, America's first financial planner, said it before she did. A penny saved is a penny…well, you know.

The key to success is establishing an amount you can comfortably save, then doing it regularly. Most experts recommend saving at least 10 percent of your annual income, but if you absolutely can't do it, don't just throw up your hands and quit. Save something—even $5 or $10 a week. And pay yourself that money before you pay anyone else. After all, you owe the most to yourself and your future.

- *Start a retirement plan.* Begin participating in your company's retirement plan, if there is one. If not, establish an Individual Retirement Account (IRA). (These are discussed in detail in chapter nine.) It doesn't matter if the ink on your diploma is still fresh or you've still got a partially used tube of acne cream in the medicine cabinet. Hard as it is to imagine, you will get older, and someday you will retire and want to live comfortably. No matter how young you are, it isn't a moment too soon to start saving for that day.

If you've already started saving regularly, be sure you are growing your money as much as you can through tax-deferred plans such as IRAs, SEPs, or 401(k)s. Since money in these retirement plans isn't taxed until you begin withdrawing it, it can grow significantly more rapidly than money in a regular investment account.

Another plus is that many larger employers now offer to match whatever you save. Make certain you are plowing as much of your savings as possible into these highly lucrative vehicles.

- *Pay cash.* Keeping credit card purchases to a minimum will help you clarify the difference between what you want and what you really need. And by using cash, you eliminate finance charges.

Axe That Debt

Debt Worksheet: Loans and Charge Accounts

You may know deep in your heart, or you may already be getting debt notices in the mail. Either way, you can start to erase the anxiety in your gut by getting an accurate picture of your debt, then taking steps to fix the problem.

Last month's payments (excluding the mortgages and credit cards you have paid off)

$_____ $_____

$_____ $_____

(Add more lines if you need to.)

1. Total monthly payments $_____

2. Your total annual disposable income divided by 12
$_____

3. Total monthly payments you can safely handle (If you are married and you and your spouse work, or if you are under 35, enter 15 percent or 20 percent of line 2.) $_____

4. Amount of room in your budget for additional debt (line 3 minus line 1) $_____

If the figure in line 4 is negative, you are in trouble. You need to modify your spending and saving habits.

- *Live on one income.* If at all possible, adjust your standard of living so that you can use one partner's paycheck for living expenses and the other partner's for savings. This rapidly builds your nest egg. It also eases the transition during rough times. If one partner loses a job, bills continue to be manageable. The only thing that you'll have to cut back on temporarily is the money you stash away.

- *Put the money from your next raise into savings.* If you earn $40,000, a 5 percent raise will give you $2,000 to sock away in a retirement account.

- *Continue to pay for debts you've already paid off.* When you finish paying off a credit card debt, car loan, or student loan, don't put the extra money back into your checking account, where it may quickly vanish. Since the expense is already factored into your budget, put the would-be payments into a mutual fund or other savings plan. And reward yourself with a gift using one of those would-be payments.

- *Eliminate one big expense a year.* If your savings have grown spotty because of other financial obligations, win back a chunk of money for your IRA by postponing a new car, a pricey vacation, or an unnecessary home repair. Fix up the old jalopy, go camping, and hang a picture over that spot on the wallpaper until next year.

GOOD DEALS

• *Consumer's Digest* magazine offers a MasterCard with an 8.8 percent interest rate for the first six months, and a 13.9 percent fixed rate later. The card also provides a 25-day **interest-free grace period** on purchases and no annual fee. For more information, call (800) 423-3273.

• KeyBank in Cleveland, Ohio, offers a KeySmart Gold card which drops your interest rate if you make **higher minimum payments** and agree to an annual fee. A KeySmart Gold card with no annual fee and a 2 percent minimum payment will charge interest at an annual rate of 17.9 percent. Users who agree to a $30 annual fee and a monthly payment that is 5 percent of your outstanding balance get a rate that drops to 8.9 percent interest a year. For more information, call (216) 689-3000.

When you substitute a cost-saving measure for a big expense, make sure that you're really saving money. If patching up your car costs $2,500, and maybe more down the road, it might make more sense to buy a new, less expensive car with a lower monthly payment—especially if you're using that credit card with the high interest rate to pay for the repairs. And if you choose to go camping instead of staying in the high-priced hotel, be sure you're not buying lots of expensive camping equipment and clothes that could cost almost as much as staying in a resort.

- *Make higher down payments*. Put as much money as you can up front on loans in order to reduce the length of the payment and save on interest payments.

- *Make your cash hard to get to*. Don't keep a lot of extra money in a savings or checking account. Put additional spare cash into a bank certificate of deposit (CD), which slaps you with penalties for early withdrawal. Be sure you really aren't going to need that cash, though. Otherwise, this plan might backfire. Also, avoid trips to the automatic teller machines—they make it just too easy to slip up.

- *Pay yourself back with interest*. When you must withdraw money from your savings account, return the borrowed money as soon as possible, plus a bit extra.

- *Reward yourself*. When you've reached your savings goal for the year, treat yourself and your family with any extra savings.

Step Five: Make More Moola

Finally, as you continue to build your savings, you'll watch your money grow. And you can use some of these ideas to further enhance your plan.

- *Moonlight*. Holding a part-time job in the evenings or on weekends is one of the best ways to bring in extra cash to put toward savings. If you have a strong skill, such as word processing or housepainting, you may be able to start your own business and take advantage of certain tax breaks for the self-employed, such as deductions associated with a home office.

Moonlighting Businesses

Seriously thinking about supplementing your income with a business of your own? Here are some ventures, most of which will earn from $5 to $20 an hour, that you can launch with an investment of a few hundred to a few thousand dollars. How much you earn depends on how much time and effort you put into it. A part-time business can pay for the "extras" your regular income cannot supply, or the cash it generates can be used for investing. And remember: Successful part-time businesses sometimes grow into full-time occupations that provide a greater income than a traditional, full-time job.

- Answering service
- Geriatric care provider
- Bill collection agency
- Gift basket maker
- Bookkeeper
- Child care service
- Kiddie chauffeur service
- Cleaning company
- Manicurist
- Closet organizer
- Moving consultant
- Delivery service
- Obedience trainer
- Dog walker
- Personal shopper

- Doll hospital
- Pet and plant sitter
- Errand service
- Proofreader
- Event planner
- Resume writing service
- Writer
- Secretarial service
- Gardener
- Tailoring service
- Housepainter
- Telephone etiquette coach
- Tutor
- Word processor

- *Have a yard sale.* This has become a popular form of recreation as well as a way to profit from junk…er, treasures…you no longer want. Some people earn hundreds, even thousands, of dollars in a day at a yard sale. Now and then, scrounge around your house for stuff that could be resold at a yard sale, and ask neighbors if they would like to join in. For larger items, such as furniture, place an advertisement in the local newspaper.

- *Make a game of bargain hunting.* By spending a few minutes a day to watch for ways to save money, you can economize on a surprising amount of stuff. Think of it as a fun challenge. Comparison shop before your buy. Clip coupons. Check out thrift stores and consignment shops, which often sell name-brand clothing for a fraction of the retail price. Get reading material at used book stores, from discount clubs, or the library rather than paying full price at chain stores.

- *Adjust your withholding.* If you get a tax refund every year, or if your income has dropped, chances are that too much in taxes is being taken from your paycheck. Talk to your employers about increasing the number of withholding exemptions as a way to increase your take-home pay.

- *Move some money into higher-interest investments.* Transfer money from a low-interest savings account into CDs or bonds. You may want to look over your portfolio with a financial planner and move a portion of your funds into more aggressive areas of growth, such as stocks.

- *Take in a roommate or boarder.* This option isn't for everyone, and precautions, such as checking references, should be taken before you accept anyone into your home. But if you have room to spare, like company, and need someone to split the living expenses, this may be the next best thing to getting married.

Credit Card Crunch

"Easy credit paves the way to bankruptcy."—Anonymous

Credit cards are like potato chips: Nobody, it seems, can ever settle for just one. They spill from our wallets; they pile up in drawers. Applications for more flow in every day with the mail, urging us to take advantage of "pre-approved" credit already set aside for our use.

Once you've reduced your debt, it's time to decide what to do about the credit cards you use. Taking your credit cards shopping is the single biggest cause of debt and the greatest threat to your financial health. Get a handle on your credit card consumption so you can concentrate on setting up your savings plan. Only then will you be able to comfortably afford the things you really want and deserve.

The 5,500 U.S. banks that issue credit cards don't really seem to care if we can pay back the debt. As far as they're concerned, if they can hook us early and keep us in debt forever, that's just fine.

Credit cards are convenient, but we pay a hefty price for that convenience. Consumer debt passed $1 trillion in 1996, and credit cards account for one-third of the total. During the holiday season, Americans go into a particular frenzy, heaping $2.8 million a minute onto their credit cards for toys, gifts, food, and clothing—and all of that with an average interest rate of 17.4 percent. The rest of the year, they are left with a financial hangover from their binge.

In addition, the more credit cards you carry, the more likely you are to experience loss or theft. And multiple credit cards means more monthly bookkeeping.

CREDIT CARD QUICKIES

• Check *Barron's National Business and Financial Weekly* for the best up-to-the-minute deals around the country.

• Bankcard Holders of America in Salem, Virginia, is another source of credit card information. Call (540) 389-5445 for a list of low-rate and no-fee cards; the charge is $4. This nonprofit organization can also send you a Personal Credit Card Payment Plan, a $15 computer program that organizes your credit cards, then details which to pay, and when, so you can end your card debt as quickly as possible.

• *The Banker's Secret Quarterly* is a newsletter that helps people get a grip on their debt. The company also sells a computer program that allows you to calculate different payment possibilities. For more information, call Good Advice Press at (800) 255-0899.

Rubbing Salt in the Wound: Hidden Fees

If you're like the average American, you're carrying $3,090 in credit card debt at 16.5 percent interest, which translates into about $475 a year in interest charges alone. If you make only the minimum payments each month, you'll be paying on that same $3,000 for more than 30 years—when your grandchildren are being born. And that's assuming you never charge another penny.

Credit card companies continue to rake in giant profits because whatever breaks they give the consumer in terms of seemingly lower interest rates or cash-back awards, they give back to themselves willy-nilly with a host of hidden fees and stunted grace periods.

There are over-the-credit-limit fees, usually $10 or $15 tacked on when you accidentally exceed your limit even by a few dollars.

There are late payment fees, also $10 to $15, which are charged when your payment arrives even a day or two after the due date printed on the monthly statement—this is in addition to the interest you're already paying. If your payment was only slightly tardy and you don't pay late on a habitual basis, try calling the customer service number and asking for a waiver. You may get lucky.

But those aren't all of the additional fees credit card issuers pay themselves.

They dip into your wallet even further with transaction charges, typically 2 to 3 percent of the total, but a maximum of $20, when you write a check against your credit card or for a cash advance. So, resist the temptation to use those "convenience checks" card issuers send you. Getting you to use them is just one more way to slap on another fee.

And let's not forget the minimum finance charge, an amount that is tacked on no matter how small your balance is, just for the heck of it. Avoid this by paying off the balance every month.

Talk the Talk

Here's some credit card lingo you need to know and some pitfalls to watch out for:

Annual Membership Fee. Use the card once and—bingo—you're considered a "member." For that privilege, you're automatically charged a fee ranging from $15 to $55, depending on the issuing company. For gold cards, annual fees can soar from $40 to $100. Avoid them like the plague.

APR. Also known as the annual percentage rate, this is the amount of interest you are charged on your purchase. But beware—the APR actually is higher than the issuing card tells you because finance charges are added to any outstanding balance and interest is compounded.

Fixed-Rate Interest. The interest rate stays the same every month unless the card issuer notifies you in advance of a change.

Grace Period. How nice. This sounds so reassuring. The grace period is the number of days you have to pay off the new balance before the credit card company adds on the finance charge. Be careful. Read the fine print to learn how long the grace period really is and whether it has changed. For example, if the issuer says you have a month's grace period, define exactly how long that is. Don't assume it means 30 or 31 days—it could be as little as 25 or even 20 days. Sometimes card issuers shrink the grace period even further by delaying when they mail the bill.

Periodic Rate. This is the rate that the card issuer applies to your outstanding account balance to figure the finance charge for each billing period.

Variable-Rate Interest. The interest rate is adjusted quarterly and is often tied to fluctuations in the prime rate. Consumers need to stay on top of these fluctuations to determine if they're getting the best deal. Check the bottom of your monthly statement to find out the amount of interest you're being charged.

Types of Cards

It pays to shop for credit cards just like you shop for anything else. There is a difference between credit cards and charge cards. Credit cards, which are sponsored by banks, retailers, oil companies, and other large corporations, let you borrow money when you don't pay off your entire balance each month. (Sometimes it's hard to remember that when you're using a credit card you're really taking out a loan.) MasterCard and Visa are credit cards. They are also known as bank cards because, until fairly recently, they were issued only through banks and other financial institutions. They offer a wide range of fees, interest rates, and conditions, depending on the card issuer.

American Express, Diner's Club, and Carte Blanche are charge cards, or travel and entertainment cards. They don't impose a credit limit and they don't charge interest. The lack of a credit limit is especially alluring to people who are taking a trip and may quickly reach their credit limit with standard bank cards. But there are sometimes "hidden" limits based on your previous patterns of spending. If you usually have a fairly low monthly balance, and you charge all your vacation expenditures, it might get questioned. If they don't allow it, you may be stuck. Unlike credit cards, charge cards do require users to pay off the whole balance every month and they may suspend the account if payment is 30 days late. If payment isn't received within 60 days, they tack on a penalty of up to $15 or 2.5 percent of the total.

Company credit cards are another form of the beast. These cards are valid only at the store or gas station issuing the card. While most of them allow a grace period and issue no annual fee, they often have extremely high interest rates—18 to 22 percent, or more, which makes them even more costly to use than standard bank cards. If you pay off these balances every month, company credit cards may be very convenient and help make bookkeeping easier. If you don't, though, you're probably getting socked with higher-than-necessary interest payments. Use your bank card instead.

Rebate cards are relative newcomers on the credit card scene. They offer consumers bonuses or cash back on a wide variety of goods and services, which can be tempting. However, you often have to charge a great deal to get even a minimal cash-back award, and rebate cards often carry a higher-than-average interest rate, which offsets the savings. You would be smarter to make a purchase using a low-rate card and spend the money you would have gotten back as a rebate on a higher quality product.

Affinity cards also are new. These are all-purpose credit cards sponsored by professional organizations, college alumni associations, and some members of the travel industry. Often, an affinity card user donates a portion of the annual fee or transaction charges to the sponsoring organization, and in return qualifies for free travel or other bonuses.

Do You Need the Fancy Stuff?

Credit card companies stay competitive by offering a host of options to consumers. If you have more than one or two credit cards, you're regularly bombarded with a confusing array of "extras"—everything from emergency roadside assistance to travel or disability insurance, coupons for merchandise or services, and extended warranties. Do you want to take advantage of them? In many cases, the extras are a lot of sizzle without a lot of steak. You'll never actually use the add-ons, or you could get better deals on the same thing elsewhere.

STRING SAVER #7

Rent rather than buy tools you will only use now and then.

One common frill that card issuers offer is price protection. This guarantees that you will pay the lowest price around for merchandise, and if you pay more, the card issuer will reimburse you. But often it's not easy to get that reimbursement. You may be required to produce a receipt along with a print ad for the same item that ran in a publication within 60 days of your purchase before your claim is considered.

Another extra consumers are offered is purchase protection, which means the issuer will reimburse you for any merchandise that is lost, stolen, or damaged within three months of purchase. You may not have any problems, but make sure you won't have to walk across burning coals to get the reimbursement. Read the fine print. Some circumstances aren't covered.

Frequent-flier miles and collision damage waivers are other common add-ons. While the collision damage may be useful if you rent cars often, the frequent-flyer miles should be approached with caution. How much do you have to charge to get the miles and, considering the interest rates and hidden fees, could you simply have paid for the ticket directly and saved money?

Finding the Best Card for You

The decision about what type of card is best for you lies in your pattern of use. First, analyze your payment strategy. Are you a "revolver"—someone who always carries balances? Or are you a "convenience user"—someone who pays off the charges every month?

Convenience users do well with charge cards, which expect and reward payment of the full balance each month. But, habitual revolvers will find only frustration and financial hardships if they use charge cards and are unable to pay the balance in full, because the issuer will punish them with late fees and may even terminate usage of the card.

Revolvers are more successful using low-interest credit cards that offer a grace period. Another aspect for revolvers to consider is how much of a balance they keep. If they always pay more than the minimum, they should look for cards that give a break on interest rates if you pay more money down.

Don't Get Scammed

Credit cards are big business in America. So is credit card fraud. One of the most common scams is the pay-per-call, 900-number telephone pitch, done either on TV or through the mail. The idea is that consumers who have poor credit or no established credit will be able to obtain a major credit card if they call the 900 number.

Most of the calls cost around $2 per minute, but sometimes the caller is charged a flat fee ranging from a few dollars to nearly $50. And rarely do the calls deliver. People often are charged money up front for a list of three or four banks offering cards with low interest rates. Sometimes they wind up with a credit card for an obscure catalogue company, which requires down payments on purchases.

Some states, such as California, regulate intrastate 900 services through the state's Public Utilities Commission. However, people operating 900 numbers from outside that state aren't subject to the laws. Until federal lawmakers establish disclosure rules and strictly regulate 900 numbers throughout the country, it's a smart idea to avoid them altogether, especially if it involves credit cards.

People who have been victims of 900-number scams should contact their U.S. senator or representative and, if direct mail solicitation was involved, the postal authorities.

If you have problems with poor or no credit, look for a bank that issues secured credit cards. Although they look like a standard bank card, secured cards have some stiff guidelines. The user must have a bank account equal to the amount of the credit limit, and it is an account the user cannot draw from. Also, interest rates and annual fees may be higher than normal, and sometimes no grace period is offered. But if payment is made promptly and the user abides by the terms, obtaining a standard bank card can eventually become a reality.

Avoid Other Forms of Credit Card Rip-Offs

- Don't give your account number in response to a phone call, postcard, or advertisement. Someone else could use the number to rack up large bills.

- Destroy your expired credit cards to prevent anyone from altering or using them. Also, cut up any other used documents that may have your credit card number on them, such as carbon copies of charge slips or receipts.

- Refuse to write your address, phone number, or Social Security number on a credit card slip. The only legal requirement is your signature.

- Don't allow merchants to charge you extra for credit-card purchases, if that practice is illegal in your state. To find out what is allowed, contact the state's division of consumer affairs, usually located within the attorney general's office, or contact the local Better Business Bureau.

When You Run into Problems

- *Billing errors.* The federal law has specific rules the credit card issuer must follow for correcting billing errors promptly. The card issuer must give you a statement describing those rules when you open an account and, after that, at least once a year. Many card issuers print a summary of your rights on each bill they send.

If you find a billing error, write a letter to the credit card company's billing address within 60 days. (For this reason you should keep credit card receipts and compare them when your bills arrive.) Include your name, your account number, the amount of the suspected error, and the reason why you believe it is an error.

The card issuer is required to look into the problem and either correct it or explain why it wasn't an error within 90 days. Until you get an answer, you don't have to pay the disputed amount.

For more information, contact Credit Billing Errors, Public Reference, Federal Trade Commission, Washington, D.C. 20580.

- *Unauthorized charges.* The federal law says that if your credit card is taken and used by someone else without your authorization—an ex-spouse, for example—you can be held liable for up to $50 per card. If you report the loss before the card is used, the law does not allow the card issuer to hold you responsible for any unauthorized charges.

If a thief uses your card before you report it missing, the most you will pay for unauthorized charges is $50. This is true even if the thief is able to use your credit card at an automated teller machine to access your credit card account.

To minimize your liability, report the loss of your card as soon as possible. Some companies have toll-free numbers printed on their statements and 24-hour service to accept emergency information.

For your own protection, follow up your phone call with a letter to the card issuer. Include your card number, when you noticed the card was missing, and the date you reported the loss.

Still Paying after All These Years

If you have a $2,000 loan and make only the minimum monthly payments, this is how long it will take you to pay off the debt.

Interest Rate	Minimum Payment	Total Interest Cost	Months to Pay Off
12.25%	2.5%	$1,141	133
17.10	2.0	3,636	298
19.80	2.0	7,636	502

*Calculations are made based on software from The Banker's Secret, P.O. Box 78, Elizaville, NY 12523, (800) 255-0899

- *Disputes about merchandise or service.* If you have a problem with merchandise or services that you charged on a credit card issued by a retailer, and you have made a good faith effort to work out the problem with that retailer, you have the right to withhold payment from the card issuer. You can withhold payment up to the amount of credit outstanding for the purchase, plus any finance or related charges.

If the card you used is a bank card, a travel and entertainment card, or another card not issued by the retailer, you can withhold payment only if the purchase was more than $50 and in your home state or within 100 miles of your billing address.

If these conditions don't apply to you, consider taking action in small claims court. This is an informal legal proceeding that is used to settle disputes up to $2,000, although in some states that limit has been raised to $5,000. Check your local telephone book under municipal, county, or state government headings for small claims court listings.

We've gone through the basics: the five steps that will get your savings plan together. Now it's time to take a look at the tools you'll use to build it. The next chapters take you through the basics of savings accounts and investments—the building blocks of your savings plan.

SAVINGS accounts, CDs, and money MARKETS

When your grandmother stashed pennies in a jar in the kitchen, she was saving. She could withdraw money from the jar any time she wanted without a penalty or loss of funds, but compounding interest did not help her money grow beyond the amount she put away. Today, low-interest savings accounts are like grandma's penny jar.

If you're still paying off debt and want to begin building your nest egg, a good old-fashioned savings account is the best way for you to get started. The major advantages are that it's safe and you can get to your money easily.

Savings Accounts

Savings accounts, which are offered by banks and credit unions, are like security blankets. Whether you decide to open a savings account through a bank or a credit union, the funds are insured—up to $100,000 total for all accounts in your name—by the Federal Deposit Insurance Corporation (FDIC) or the National Credit Union Association (NCUA). That reduces the risk of losing money, as you could with other investments.

Despite their generally low rate of interest (as little as 2 percent, in some cases) savings accounts are convenient. It is a simple matter to open a savings account and, when you have a few spare dollars, go to the bank and deposit them, without the hassle of going through a broker or agent, as with other, more complicated investments. Also, the money is easily withdrawn without fear of penalties, unless your bank requires a minimum balance. In addition, you can easily see from your savings statement or passbook exactly how much money you have at any given moment, information that is not so readily available with other types of investments.

Insured means that, should the bank undergo a financial crisis because of mismanagement or be destroyed by a natural disaster, depositers will be reimbursed for any financial loss, up to $100,000. Those who deposit money in a bank that is not FDIC-insured, however, could wind up losing everything. To be safe, always put your money in a bank that is FDIC-insured.

The FDIC was originated in the early 1930s, when banks were failing because of the Depression. Yes, banks have failed since then, and people have gotten their money back, if the bank was FDIC-insured. As long as the institution is insured by the FDIC and you have less than $100,000 in accounts, your money is protected. If you have $100,000 in one account and $100,000 in another account, both at the same bank, both will be insured by the FDIC if they are separate accounts under different names. For example, George and Jen Robinson may have a $100,000 account under both names; George may have another in his name only; Jen may have one in her name only. All three will be insured. To be very safe, however, don't put all of your eggs in one basket. Open three $100,000 accounts in three different banks.

To find out if your bank is insured by the FDIC, look for a sign or a plaque in the bank that says so. Banks that are insured typically are eager to let consumers know. If you don't see any signs that mention FDIC coverage, ask the bank manager before opening an account.

If a bank should fail, federal regulators take control of the assets and depositers are reimbursed. If your bank is not insured, you should be worried, because your money is vulnerable. Switch to a bank that is backed by the FDIC.

The biggest drawback to savings accounts is that lower yields often don't allow you to keep ahead of the inflation rate, which gobbles up your money almost as soon you deposit it. But they are perfect places to save money while you're paying off debt, setting your priorities, and making the choices that will allow you to get enough money to invest in higher yield instruments.

If you choose to use a savings account as one of your primary modes of stashing cash, or if you plan to use it as a parking place for sums that later will be disbursed to other types of investments, you should know a bit about them.

There are two main types of accounts. Passbook accounts give the account holder a small book that records your balance with every transaction, along with the payment of interest by the bank. Statement accounts provide account holders with a monthly or quarterly statement rather than a passbook. Usually the bank decides which one you get. If you have a preference, they may accommodate you—if they won't, it may be a reason to choose a different bank.

BANK ON THE BLINK?

Veribanc, a bank rating service based in Wakefield, Massachusetts, provides information on the stability of banks. For a $10 safety rating of your bank, call (617) 245-8370. Another option is to call the Office of Consumer Affairs, which oversees the Federal Deposit Insurance Corporation (FDIC), at (202) 393-8400.

The mechanics of the accounts are relatively simple. You give the bank your money, it holds on to it for as long as you like, and the bank pays you interest. When you want to make a deposit, you go to the bank (or a branch), fill out a deposit slip, and hand the money to a teller. If it's a passbook account, the bank records the deposit in the passbook. If it's a statement account, you get a receipt at the time you make the deposit; you should keep your receipts to check against the statement to be sure there are no errors. If you want to make a withdrawal, you go to the bank (or a branch), hand the teller your passbook or withdrawal slip (for a statement account), and the teller gives you the money, recording the transaction in the passbook or giving you a receipt. Most savings accounts come with ATM cards which can be used to make deposits and withdrawals.

How Very Interesting

One of the best parts about a savings account is that you get to watch your money earn that interest. But remember: It is just as important for consumers to shop around for a bank as it is to shop for the best mutual fund or financial planner. Taking your money to the bank down the street may be convenient, but it may not be the smartest move financially. You cannot assume that all banks offer the same rates of interest, the same way of calculating interest, the same services, or the same fees and penalties.

Almost all savings accounts earn at least some minimum amount of interest. You should ask about interest before you open the account, though, to be sure the bank offers it—there's no law that requires banks to do this.

Some banks require a minimum balance; others do not. Check with your bank before you open the account. Be realistic about whether or not you will be able to maintain a minimum balance if one is required. If you don't think you can, look for another bank or type of account that doesn't require one, because you will pay a penalty if your account drops below the minimum balance. The rules regulating these are fairly exhaustive and vary from bank to bank. Check with your bank to learn the rules that apply to that particular institution.

Banks have different methods of computing interest. When Jefferson Bank trumpets that it compounds interest, that means its customers are earning interest on the interest that already has been paid to them, as well as on their balance. When Hayes Bank says that its pays "simple" interest, it means they pay only on your balance and not on any interest that has accrued.

Obviously, compounding interest is going to be a better deal. A rate of 4 percent paid once a year is a straight 4 percent, or $40 on a $1,000 balance. But the rate of 4 percent paid to you in compound interest is going to be higher, depending on how often it is compounded, because it will include interest on the $1,000 plus the previous interest earned. The larger your savings and the longer you leave the sum to compound, the more you will have.

Ken and Elaine, a couple in their early 20s with two young children, had little money to spare for saving. They decided to set a goal of saving just $5 a week, which they put into an account earning 5 percent interest compounded quarterly. Within one year, they had $266.45; within five years, $1,475.10; and within ten years, $3,366.23.

Compare that with what they would have earned had they put the same amount into an account bearing 5 percent in straight interest. After one year, they would have $260; after five years, $1,300; and after ten years, $2,600.

If interest is compounded monthly or daily, the results are even better. Banks can boost the return a bit more using math tricks. One of those is called 360-day compounding and is used by several high yielders. Institutions that compound daily divide the interest rate by 365 and compound it for 365 days. Institutions that use 360-day compounding divide the rate by 360 and compound it for 365 days. The extra five days make a difference. For example, the usual yield on a rate of 5 percent compounded daily is 5.13 percent. But if the same 5 percent is compounded on a 360-day basis, the yield rises to 5.20.

Savings accounts start to earn interest at different times, depending on the bank. You'll want to look for a bank that pays interest from the day of deposit to the day of withdrawal, so you will earn interest on every dollar, every day. Other banks pay interest on what is called an "average daily balance." This method will pay you interest only on the smallest balance you have in your account during the interest period. In some cases, you will earn a lower rate if your balance drops below a minimum.

It's important for you to know when interest is credited to your account. Check your passbook or your statements to see if the payments are made at the end of a quarter, the beginning of the month, or during a particular month. Many institutions have a policy that states if you withdraw funds before the stated interest payment date, you will lose all the interest owed on those funds for that interest period. If your bank has that rule, try to schedule your withdrawal immediately after the date the interest is credited to your account.

You might also ask the bank if there is a grace period around the payment date when you can withdraw money so you don't get zapped by a loss of interest. This swings the other way, too. Ask if there is a grace period when you can deposit money and be paid interest for that period.

Some banks penalize customers for making frequent withdrawals. They also may charge a monthly or quarterly fee of about $5 a month if your balance dips below a required minimum.

Also, before you open an account, it's a good idea to consider banks that have branch locations that are convenient for you, either close to where you work or live, and that are open when you need them to be. Although banks are traditionally open from 9 a.m. to 3 p.m., Monday through Friday, almost all of them now have extended hours on some days, and may even be open part of Saturday.

Some banks offer services by phone that include accessing information about account balances, transferring funds from one account to the other, and even applying for loans.

How to Open a Savings Account

After you've done your homework and chosen the bank that works best for you, take your cash or checkbook, and walk right in. Head for the desks, not the tellers' windows, and tell the clerk you want to open an account. At that point you may be asked if you want an account that requires a minimum balance (it will pay a slightly higher interest rate). You sign some papers, give them your Social Security number, hand over the money, and you're set.

Certificates of Deposit

Certificates of deposit are "safe" places to put money and are relatively free of investment risk. A certificate of deposit is a loan to a bank. When you make a deposit, you are loaning the bank money for a designated period of time; for the privilege of using your money, the bank pays you interest. CDs differ from savings accounts in that there is a time limit during which the depositer agrees not to withdraw the funds. Because your money is tied up for this period of time, the bank offers a greater rate of interest than on a savings account.

Banks determine the size of a CD, the length of time they are offered, and the interest rate. Typically, interest rates on CDs are tied to fluctuations in the stock market and the prime interest rate. However, banks determine what interest rates they want to offer, based on those factors as well as what competitors are offering. Before opening a CD, shop around for the best rates. Local newspapers often publish those rates; you also can call banks directly.

Like standard savings accounts, CDs are offered by banks and credit unions, and the funds are insured. And like passbook loans, interest on CDs may be paid as simple interest or compounded interest, and be paid during specified periods.

But there are differences. In most cases, a fairly large deposit is required to open a CD. Depending on the bank, you may need $500 or more, but denominations can range as high as $5,000 to $10,000.

AVOID YOUR ATM

Automatic teller machines can be serious temptations if you're trying to save money. They make withdrawing and spending money just too easy. Many also tack on a service charge for each transaction, and in some areas they have become a paradise for muggers.

Plan ahead, and withdraw cash directly from your bank. Having to make a trip to the bank each time you want some extra cash may limit your number of withdrawals, and your personal safety won't be in jeopardy.

Interest rates on CDs can be fixed—meaning they stay the same for the term of the deposit, no matter how much it fluctuates otherwise. Rates can also be variable—rising and falling with the prime rate. If you choose a variable rate CD, be sure that it offers you a high minimum interest rate.

Funds cannot be withdrawn from a CD account for a designated time period—anywhere from a month to five years—without a penalty and a reduction in interest. At some banks you could lose all the interest no matter when you make an early withdrawal. Most banks, however, give you a little more leeway. For example, on 3-, 6-, and 12-month CDs, you might lose 3 months' interest if you withdraw the funds before the maturity date.

STRING SAVER #8

Do your grocery shopping only once a week. The less you are exposed to temptation, the less likely you are to give in to it.

CD holders need to keep their eyes open for maturity notices that arrive in the mail. If you fail to tell the bank what you want done with the CD, the bank will automatically roll over, or reinvest, the account and you won't be able to withdraw from it, penalty-free, for another several months or years.

In general, the longer your money stays in the CD, the more you earn. If you want to keep a significant amount of money in CDs, vary the maturity dates. If interest rates drop, some of your CDs still will be producing excellent yields. If rates go up, you have funds to reinvest at the new yields.

In addition to banks and credit unions, brokerage houses also sell CDs, which are federally insured. The benefit of buying from a broker rather than your local bank is that the broker can shop around the country for the best rates and terms.

You can find out what local institutions offer the best rates by reading the CD rate table in the business section of your local newspaper. Individuals who choose not to use a broker can find out who has the highest paying CDs in the country by reading national newspapers such as *The Wall Street Journal,* or financial publications such as *Barron's.*

No matter where your money is located, you can make deposits, withdrawals, transfer funds, or open new CDs by mail or phone. The steps are easy:

• Most banks and credit unions have toll-free numbers.

- When you call the institution, ask for the person who supervises personal accounts or ask for the "national desk," which deals only with out-of-town customers. Tell the representative how much you have to invest and that you are interested in opening a CD account. Be sure to mention the CD length you want.

Ask for the following information:

- The latest interest rate and how interest is calculated

- When your interest earnings will begin

- An account form for your CD. When it arrives, make a copy of all documents, especially the signature card, which is your definitive proof of ownership should the institution fail.

If you choose to open an account by mail, you can have an application mailed or faxed to you to complete. You'll probably have to send copies of proper identification.

A key advantage of making a transaction by mail is, of course, convenience. No running back and forth to a bank, fighting traffic, using gas. In addition, since you have shopped around, you are getting a better deal at this bank than at a local facility. The drawback is, as so many of us have experienced, the mail itself. Envelopes can easily be lost. If you are concerned about your check disappearing into the great postal void, go to your post office and have them send it by return certified mail; that way, you will be notified when the bank receives your transaction.

Your purchase should be posted the same day, unless it arrives after the bank's cut-off time, often 3 p.m. In that case, the transaction will be posted the next day. Make your check payable to the institution, not an individual, and endorse it "for deposit only." If the institution does not provide account-opening documents, draft a letter specifying how much you are depositing, the account type and term, the account number, rate, what the interest will yield, and the check amount. Make sure you include your name, address, and phone number.

Money Market Accounts and Funds

Like a CD or a savings account, a money market account is another means of saving money "safely" because the funds are insured by the FDIC and a bank sets the interest rate. In addition to low risk, the principal attraction of money market accounts is that they pay slightly higher interest rates than passbook accounts, perhaps as much as half a percentage point.

But they usually require a minimum deposit of $1,000 or more, and fees may be charged if the account falls below a minimum balance. Money market accounts do permit you to write a maximum of three checks on the account, and withdrawals are limited to six per month. If you go over the limit, there is a fee.

STRING SAVER #9

Rent movies instead of going out to the theater. You also can buy **previewed videos,** swap movies with friends, or check them out of the local library. If you want to go to the theater, head for discount movie houses or take in a matinee, when admission is lower. When you're there, avoid buying high-priced snacks. Eat before you go.

Money market accounts should not be confused with money market mutual funds. A money market fund is a pool of money invested by an investment company in commercial paper (company-issued debt used to finance short-term needs), Treasury bills, certificates of deposit, and similar short-term instruments. A money fund strives to return 98 percent of its profits to shareholders and keep its share price at $1. Because of these regulations, money funds are considered the least risky of mutual funds, but they are not insured by the FDIC. They are protected by the Securities Investor Protection Corporation (SIPC), but only if the brokerage goes out of business—not if market fluctuations cause the value of the investment to decline.

In exchange for investors giving up that insurance, these funds typically pay more interest than bank money market accounts, although they are very short-term investments with a relatively low rate of return. Since a money market fund is a type of mutual fund, it is administered by a fund manager. You can find out about money

market funds from financial planners, brokers, and banks that sell them. (See chapter four for more information about mutual funds.)

Credit Unions

Rather than putting their money into banks, 70.4 million Americans today choose to do business with credit unions. A credit union is a nonprofit financial institution owned by its members, who are also the shareholders. Credit unions are formed by people with a common bond. They may work for the same employer, belong to the same union, or even live in a defined geographical area. Before a group of shareholders can form a credit union, they must go through an application process and adhere to governmental regulations. If the credit union is granted a charter, the funds within the institution are protected by the National Credit Union Association, just like funds deposited in a bank are insured by the FDIC.

Credit unions are attractive because they offer an array of banking services such as checking and savings accounts, automobile loans, mortgages, Individual Retirement Accounts (IRAs), certificates of deposit, and almost any other service your bank would provide. A few credit unions even offer stock brokerage services. The advantages are that because they are nonprofit organizations, they often provide lower rates for mortgages and loans, and higher yields on CDs and savings accounts than banks. The disadvantage is that you must be within the field of membership—an employee of a particular business, for example—to be able to join.

STRING SAVER #10

Attend free investment seminars. Reputable investment firms often offer workshops that provide valuable advice because they're hoping you become a client. But you're under no obligation to do business with them, and you might just learn something. What have you got to lose?

You can use a credit union instead of a bank—many people do. Or you can go à la carte, using some of the credit union's services and some of the bank's. You'll need to do some comparison shopping between the bank and credit union of your choice to see which can offer you the best deals on various services.

STOCKS, bonds, and mutual FUNDS

Everyone talks about investing—on television, in print, around the coffee machine at work. There's such a continual flood of information, in fact, that it all begins to sound like a lot of babble. But one message does come through. Investing is something most people should be doing.

This doesn't mean that you should rush out and toss your life savings into an investment because you heard that a friend of a friend's uncle made a killing on it. Investing is like swimming: You don't just jump into the pool without knowing how to do it or you'll wind up getting hurt. Dip your toes in first, then get in gradually and safely. Learn before you leap.

What Is Investing?

Investing is not the same as saving. If you keep your money in savings accounts, you can get to it whenever you want to, but it doesn't take advantage of high interest rates. Often the growth of savings accounts does not keep pace with the rate of inflation, so by keeping funds in them for years, you actually end up losing money in the long run.

Investing takes a more long-term, aggressive approach to growing your money using a variety of alternatives, including stocks, bonds, mutual funds, money market accounts, and certificates of deposit (CDs). Although your money grows more quickly than in a "safer" savings account, you do face more of a risk of losing money as the economy fluctuates.

STRING SAVER #11

Check your refrigerator for energy efficiency. Refrigerators represent about 30 percent of most electric bills. Open the door and place a dollar bill against the seal, then close the door. If you can remove the bill easily, the seal needs to be replaced.

Risky Business

In a nutshell, investing is a lot like romance with its seesaw of risks and returns. To get something back, you have to take a chance. In investing parlance, a return is the amount of money you earn from an investment. Risks are those factors that make the amount of your return uncertain. How each will balance out is part of the endless, exquisitely excruciating game of investing. In general, though, the lower level of risk involved with an investment, the lower your potential return will be; the greater the risk, the greater potential return—but also the greater chance for loss.

On the financial superhighway, there are a lot of side roads you could turn into. Your priority at this point in your travels is to investigate some investment avenues—Wall Street, Bond Street, and Mutual Fund Way—because stocks, bonds, and mutual funds are the means to effect some major savings. This route is becoming more and more popular as people realize it's impossible to win the race against inflation by keeping money in savings accounts and less risky securities such as money market funds and certificates of deposit. Because of inflation, you end up losing money in the long run if you keep it all in these kinds of investments.

According to a January 12, 1997 article in *The New York Times,* the Standard & Poor's 500, an index that measures stock performance, earned a total return of 22.9 percent in 1996. This compares to the 2.5 percent average return you can expect from bank savings accounts, 3.62 percent from money market accounts, and 5.29 percent from one-year CDs.

All this translates to real dollars in your pocket when you invest in stocks, bonds, and mutual funds—real dollars that add up to more savings to give you greater security, more peace of mind, more disposable income, and ultimately, more resources to live the life you want and deserve. Saving through stocks, bonds, and mutual funds is exciting and fun, too, because the world of investing can be fast-paced and full of surprises.

While greater numbers of people are investing in stocks, bonds, and mutual funds, many people are missing tremendous opportunities, largely because they don't know enough about them. If you're feeling clueless, too, don't give up. This chapter will show you the ABCs of stocks, bonds, and mutual funds and how investing in them can get you started on the road to big savings. And because learning how to use these investment instruments to your best advantage is an ongoing work-in-progress, you'll find the tools here that will help you stay informed to make the right decisions.

The Stock Market

You've heard the stories. The stock market plunges dramatically, and in the blink of an eye, people lose thousands of dollars. Part of the legend of the Great Depression is the image of Wall Street businessmen jumping from office building windows. There are true stories of stock market investors who took fatal leaps after losing everything in one day. This hardly makes investing in stocks sound very enticing. If there's so much risk involved, why does anyone get into the market in the first place?

Like bungee jumping, investing in the stock market can be full of thrills, but it's all ups and downs. You might be saying to yourself, "I wouldn't go bungee jumping, so why would I invest my hard-earned dollars in the stock market?" It is a good idea to be cautious. In fact, caution, along with education, a long-term outlook, and diversification, is the key to being successful in the stock market. You have to be willing to take the time to educate yourself about the market before you dive in, and once you are there, you need to stay informed about your investments so that you will know when it's time to make changes to your portfolio. There are plenty of investment professionals you can turn to for help on the education and information fronts, and you should do so.

Getting involved in the stock market can be a golden opportunity for you to put whatever assets you have to work, earning you more money over the long haul. But be prepared for the long haul. The stock market isn't a quick financial fix. You have to be prepared to ride out the dips in the market if you expect to realize any significant return on your investments. Never invest money that you need for daily living expenses or short-term goals, such as making a down payment on a car.

Is investing in the stock market risky? You betcha. But you should only take risks that you can live with. Never invest in something that's going to keep you awake at night. But even more importantly, diversify your investments so that your money is in several different types of investments of varying risk levels and in different industries. That way, the performance of any one investment won't make or break your portfolio.

STRING SAVER #12

Go to skating rinks, roller rinks, swimming pools, bowling alleys, and other recreational facilities at off-peak times, when rates often are lower.

Before investing, determine your objectives. Do you want to make money for income or are you investing to meet a goal, such as funding your retirement? There are different types of investments that are best to meet different needs. Then, choose a reputable broker to work with you to meet your objectives. Always keep informed about how your money is being invested and add more stocks to your portfolio slowly, or as you feel comfortable.

Getting Professional Help

If you are new to the stock market, you shouldn't try to go it alone. Find yourself a broker you trust. There are basically three types of brokers: full-service, discount, and deep-discount. Which kind of broker you go with depends on how much and what kind of service you want.

- *Full-service brokers.* A full-service broker is typically employed by full-service brokerage firms such as Merrill Lynch or Paine Webber. He may also be an independent financial adviser who has a "seat" on the exchange and is therefore able to directly execute orders for himself and his clients. You'll pay more for a full-service broker, but you'll also get the most help from one. He'll be able to provide you with extensive information, investment guidance, and long-term financial planning. If you need someone to help you decide when and what to buy and sell, then a full-service broker is for you. You'll pay the highest commissions to a full-service broker (up to 75 percent higher than at a discount broker), but the handholding you receive will usually be well worth it.

- *Discount brokers.* It's less expensive to buy and sell stocks through a discount broker than it is to work with full-service brokers. Of course, as with any "cheaper" product or service, you get what you pay for. Discount brokerage firms offer far less service and information than full-service brokerages, and because of this you'll have to do more of your own research. Examples of discount brokerage firms are OLDE Discount Brokerage and Charles Schwab.

- *Deep-discount brokers.* These brokers are the least expensive, and they will not hold your hand. Most of these firms offer only the most remedial level of service, such as quarterly statements and maybe an 800 number to call to place orders. Some of these firms operate only by computer so that you can only place your orders by contacting the firm through the Internet or another computer network. If you are willing to make your own choices and your own mistakes without having someone there to advise you, this may be your best bet.

Stock Savvy

- Get informed and stay informed. Read the business section of the local paper and/or *The Wall Street Journal*. Get online and check out the financial-related Web sites, home pages, and business resources on the Internet and America Online.

- Never buy stocks indiscriminately, just because you have some spare cash to burn off.

- Ignore your broker's so-called hot tips. If the tip is so hot, chances are many people have heard about it besides you. This is clear when the stock has already been moving, which means that insiders have been buying long before you and everyone else got the tip. After you buy, when the news becomes "public," who will be left to buy?

- Don't be a slave to trends. Look where others have not. It's possible for the price of stocks of some small- and mid-sized companies to double within a three-year period while their earnings grow at 25 percent a year. These stocks often are being ignored by Wall Street but have the potential to be excellent performers, if you get into the game early. But beware: Finding these companies is sometimes a matter of luck, and investing in them is more risky than investing in industry leaders.

- Track a stock's record before you buy, and check *The Value Line Investment Survey* for additional information. *Value Line*, available in many libraries, offers rankings, descriptions, and evaluations of more than 1,500 stocks.

- Look close to home. Knowing about solid but relatively unknown companies that are starting in your own backyard puts you in a good position to become an investor. Beware of becoming emotionally involved in these companies, though. Don't be shy about researching them as thoroughly as you would scrutinize strangers.

- Study the company's balance sheet and attend annual meetings of nearby companies. Learn how cash is being spent and how the company plans to meet its objectives. Run from companies that have a lot of debt or unresolved internal problems. Be wary of those that offer "creative" excuses for underachievement.

- Keep turnover to a minimum. Be selective about your purchases to begin with and hold tight during inevitable business cycle bumps. However, if you aren't satisfied with a stock's performance after two consecutive years, sell it.

- Over 1,000 companies offer investors dividend reinvestment plans. These allow you to reduce broker commissions, because the dividends are automatically reinvested without her help. In some cases, you may be offered a discount on these additional shares. Remember, though, that if you are reinvesting for income, this may not be the best approach because you will stop receiving dividend checks. In addition, you will be required to pay income taxes on the reinvested dividends just as if you had received them and cashed them in.

- Don't expect immediate gratification. The stock market fluctuates—there are continuous ups and downs. The people who do best in the market are those who hang in there for the long haul.

- If it sounds too good to be true, it probably is.

The difference between going to a full-service broker and a discount broker is like the difference between going to a good clothing store or buying from a catalogue. Maybe you'll get a good deal from the catalogue; maybe the clothing will fit when you get it. Then again, maybe not. Your financial goals should dictate the choice of a broker. A do-it-yourself investor who chooses a discount firm is someone who wants to save money on commissions and is willing to take the time to research the market regularly.

STRING SAVER #13

Buy classic styles of medium-weight clothing that you can layer and wear almost every season, year after year.

Choosing a Good Broker

Finding a good stockbroker is a little like finding a good doctor. Talk to other investors in financial circumstances similar to yours to see who they recommend. Look in the ads in financial newspapers like *The Wall Street Journal* and the business sections of large metropolitan newspapers like *The New York Times*. A comprehensive reference source is Standard & Poor's *Directory of Security Dealers in North America*, a who's who of 14,455 broker/dealers listed alphabetically by state, city, and specialty. It's available in most public libraries or from Standard & Poor's, 65 Broadway, New York, NY 10006, (800) 221-5277.

And don't forget online sources. Even if you don't plan to do any trading online, you can get lots of informaton by checking the sites of brokers that maintain Web sites or forums on AOL. Here are a few to get you started:

Resource	Where to Find It
Closing Bell (for customized investment information)	http://www.merc.com/cbell2.html
Fidelity Investments	AOL's Personal Finance
Merrill Lynch	AOL's Personal Finance
PAWWS Financial Network	http://www.pawws.secapl.com/
Vanguard Group	AOL's Personal Finance
T. Rowe Price	AOL's Personal Finance

Once you've narrowed your selection down to a few candidates, it might be helpful to consult the National Association of Securities Dealers (NASD), a self-regulatory organization of the securities industry, which maintains an electronic file of brokers which have violated securities regulations. If any of your potential brokers appear in this file, scratch the name off fast. You don't need to start a relationship with doubts. Contact NASD at 1735 K Street NW, Washington, DC, 20006, or call (202) 728-6900.

Interviewing Potential Brokers

Before selecting a stockbroker, interview potential candidates. Here are some questions to ask:

- Where did you study? What did you study?

- How long have you been with the brokerage firm? What was your previous employment, and why did you leave?

- What is your source of investment recommendations?

- Will I have access to the firm's research department?

- How do you get paid? Do you get higher commissions from recommending certain securities over others?

- How often will you provide me with statements and reports about how my stocks are performing, and how extensive will the reports be?

- Can you provide client references?

FULL-SERVICE VERSUS DISCOUNT COMMISSIONS

A client who purchases 100 shares of stock for $10 each pays a $37.50 commission at **Quick & Reilly,** one of the largest discount brokerages in the country, and from $47 to $50 at a full-service brokerage.

If the client buys 500 shares of stock at $15, the commission is $77.75 at Quick & Reilly, and from $101 to $205 at a full-service brokerage. **Ceres Securities,** a deep-discount broker, charges a flat rate of $18 per trade for U.S. stocks.

When you invest in the stock market through a broker, your investment is protected by Securities Investor Protection Corporation (SIPC), a government-sponsored organization funded by its member brokerage firms. Coverage is for cash and securities in your account for up to $500,000—cash losses are limited to $100,000—if, and only if, the brokerage goes out of business. (This insurance is similar to what the FDIC does for bank savings accounts.) You are not covered if the companies the brokerage invested your money in go out of business. That kind of risk is inherent to investing in the stock market, and nobody can protect you from it. If your brokerage does go out of business, report any losses to your state securities commission, which will help with reimbursement.

STRING SAVER #14

Buy mix-and-match styles rather than dresses. You'll be able to add to your wardrobe piece by piece, as items go on sale.

Stocks 101

When you buy stock in a company, you become an owner in that company. For example, if you buy a share of stock in your favorite sneaker company, you buy a part of its facility, its product, and everything it owns. As an owner you get to share in the profits of the company, and you also share in the risks of doing business. If the company has 10,000 shares of stock and you own 100, then you own 1 percent of the company.

There are two ways to make money in the stock market: by receiving a share of the profits in the form of dividends and by realizing capital gains by selling your stock for more than you paid for it.

As an owner, you may get to share in the profits of the company through the receipt of dividends. If the company generates a profit and distributes that to its stockholders, you receive a share of that distribution in the form of a dividend. The more shares you own, the larger your dividend will be, and since that dividend is considered income, you will be responsible for paying taxes on it at the same rate as any other income you receive. Not all companies pay dividends, especially those that don't earn a profit.

In some cases, investors depend on dividends as the major source of income from their stocks. Traditionally, these people have been retirees, widows, recipients of trust funds, and other stockholders who choose not to tamper with the principal. But there are other people who look at any dividends they receive as icing on the cake. Most likely, any large rates of return that you earn from the stock market will come when the share price of a stock you own appreciates and you sell it to realize a capital gain. The value of stock is a simple case of supply and demand. Once a company has sold its initial batch of stock to the public and the stock is being traded on the market, the value is determined by what investors are willing to pay for it and what sellers are willing to accept. If a company is doing well in the marketplace, more people are going to want to buy the stock and the value of that stock will rise. If you sell the stock for a higher price than you paid for it, you win.

If you realize capital gains from the sale of stock, you need to declare it to the IRS and you will have to pay taxes on it, just as you pay taxes on any income you receive. The good news is that you don't pay taxes on your stocks as they rise in value—only when you sell them for a profit or receive dividends.

Creating Your Portfolio

To create the portfolio that's right for you, there are several factors you need to think about in addition to your goals and your tolerance for risk. Age is a key consideration; the younger you are, the more aggressively you can invest. If the stock market plummets, you have plenty of time to sit tight and wait until it rises again to make up the shortfall. If you're close to retirement, however, the losses will have a greater impact on your financial picture and your plans.

STRING SAVER #15

When you're shopping for a new car, go to the dealership at the end of the day when the exhausted salespeople may be less inclined to engage in lengthy haggling. Also, head to dealerships at the end of the month. Salespeople have a quota to make. If yours hasn't made his yet, you could be looking at a desperate soul more eager to make a deal in your favor. Around Christmas, when few people are buying new cars, the salespeople can be especially amenable.

Marital status comes into play when you are creating an overall investment strategy. People with children will need more money than those without. Investments can help fund the expenses that pop up along the way, such as paying for braces and summer camp. They also can help replenish your depleted savings when Junior finally is off on his own. Income and spending habits play a critical role in the formation of the investment portfolio. People with less income and a modest amount of savings probably should not invest more than a fraction of their funds in individual stocks and bonds. Those with greater income will be able to handle more risk. And if you're the type of person who is prone to racking up large bills, you would be well served by vehicles that allow you to get your hands on cash quickly rather than investing in assets such as real estate or artwork, which cannot be turned into cash fast.

Buy Different Stocks in Different Types of Companies to Meet Different Investment Goals

Here's a basic list of goals and the types of stocks that match them. Talk with your financial planner or full-service broker about which would be the best for you.

- *Supplement your income.* If you are looking for a stable monthly return to supplement your income, go with some income stocks. They are issued by companies in fairly stable, financially healthy industries, such as utilities. Income stocks are known to pay a substantial portion of their earnings in dividends and are favored by retirees and others who need regular dividend income, because the performance of such stocks is somewhat reliable.

- *Long-term appreciation.* If you are looking for stocks that will earn you some significant bucks over the long haul, go with some growth stocks. They pay little or nothing in dividends, but the price of the stock can rise more in value than other stocks; it also can drop, depending on the fortunes of the company.

- *Stability.* If you are looking for relatively safe and stable stocks that will grow gradually over the long haul, your best bet is the blue chips. Named after the poker chip with the highest value, these stocks are usually reliable and are issued by solid, well-established companies that are dominant in their industries. Because these companies are less vulnerable to market swings, they are less likely to sway during market cycles, and investors in these companies tend to enjoy steady dividends in the best and the worst of times.

- *Reap the benefits of a bull market.* If you want your investments to increase in value along with a rising stock market, go with cyclical stocks. But keep in mind that these stocks are likely to fall if the market begins to drop. These stocks are issued by companies with high profitability during particular seasons or periods, such as those in the housing industry. The value of the stock drops sharply during the "off" period. Because of this, the investor needs to time transactions carefully, which for a novice may be too tricky.

- *Go for a wild joyride.* If you are in the market for that adrenaline rush associated with daredevil acts like riding a roller coaster, take a chance on speculative stocks: But be forewarned—you could end up losing your shirt. The cost of these stocks typically is high when compared with the company's earnings, the value of the stock fluctuates, and there is a good chance you'll lose most or all of your investment. Success with speculative stocks comes only with expertise and a lot of luck. Think of it as gambling and allocate only a small portion of your investment portfolio to these kinds of stocks.

Selecting Individual Stocks

Once you've chosen a broker and decided the mix of stocks you want to achieve proper diversification and to meet your investment goals, it's time to make your actual selections. Even if you're dealing with a full-service broker whose recommendations you trust, you should do some of your own research before taking her advice. There really is no quick way to do this, no surefire list of great stocks to pick. It's a matter of educating yourself about what's out there and making intelligent, informed decisions.

The first thing to do before you even think about selecting stocks is to become an avid reader and listener. Read the news sections of financial newspapers like *The Wall Street Journal, Barron's, Investor's Business Daily,* and the financial sections of your closest major metropolitan newspapers. Read business-oriented magazines like *BusinessWeek, Kiplinger's, Forbes, Fortune, Money,* and *Inc.* Pay attention to business segments of radio and TV news broadcasts, and listen to business radio networks like Bloomberg and Business News Network.

A very useful specialized publication is *The Value Line Investment Survey.* It comes out weekly, is in most public libraries, and has an overview of the stock market and recommendations and reviews of particular stocks.

Another terrific tool is the American Association of Individual Investors (AAII), an independent, nonprofit organization that provides information and resources to investors. It offers seminars, publications, educational videos, and a newsletter. It also maintains a presence on America Online's Personal Finance Center with all sorts of valuable material, including information on financial/retirement planning, stock selection, managing your portfolio, dealing with your broker, computerized investing, and international investing. While you're in the neighborhood, the rest of AOL's Personal Finance section is a gold mine to explore. You could spend a good deal of time going from link to link, absorbing amazing amounts of information. Here's what you'll find on AOL's Personal Finance:

- American Express ExpressNet

- AOL's Your Business

- Bizinsider

- Personal Finance Chat Rooms

- Business News

- Company News

- Company Research

- Disclosure 10-Ks/10-Qs & Financial Statements

- Dow Jones Business Center

- First Call Earnings Estimates

- Hoover's Company Profiles

- *Inc.* Magazine Online

- Investor's Exchange

- Investors' Network

- Market News

- MoneyWhiz

- Morningstar Stock & Fund Reports

- The Motley Fool: Stocks

- The Nightly Business Report

- Quotes & Portfolios

- Wall Street SOS Forum

- *Worth* Online

- Your Business Lunch

AOL's Financial Newsstand is a convenient place to browse online versions of financial publications like *BusinessWeek, Investment News, Investor's Business Daily, The New York Times, Chicago Tribune,* and *Crain's.*

SOMEONE TO WATCH OVER YOU—SECURITIES AND EXCHANGE COMMISSION

The Securities and Exchange Commission is an independent, nonpartisan federal agency that protects U.S. investors against malpractice in the securities markets. The Securities Act of 1933 requires anyone offering securities for sale to file a registration statement with the SEC disclosing pertinent financial information, including the securities holdings of their officers and directors.

The SEC's jurisdiction includes the stock exchanges, broker-dealers, and mutual funds and enforces the federal securities laws. It investigates possible violations and has the power to recommend appropriate action.
The SEC also serves as adviser to federal courts in corporate bankruptcy proceedings.

Online Trading

Want to trade stocks online? Visit one of these World Wide Web sites and bring the broker into your living room.

Ceres Securities   Web site: http://www.ceres.com/

E*TRADE   Web site: http://www.etrade.com/

Lombard   Web site: http://www.lombard.com/

PAWWS Financial Network   Web site: http://pawws.secapl.com/

PC Financial Network   America Online; Keyword PCFN

Schwab Online   Web site: http://www.schwab.com/

TradePlus   America Online; Keyword TradePlus

Initially, you may find yourself spending hours poring over these types of resources, but soon, you'll learn to sift through the massive amounts of information available to pull out just what's relevant to your situation. Exposure to this media will give you a sense of market trends, news about exciting new companies, and general information about the economy. It may all sound like gibberish at first, but you'll be surprised at how much insight you can gain by just putting yourself in the way of the information flow.

Once you feel a little more informed and a bit more savvy, it's time to start thinking about individual stocks. What sounds interesting? What new companies are out there? Make a list of the companies that sound like dynamic and possibly lucrative investments. Now you need to do some nitty-gritty research on them.

Get Out Your Magnifying Glass

In order to determine whether or not a company has the right to use your money, you need to be a detective and investigate it as much as you can. Check out its earnings, its dividends, how the various surveys and reports rate its stock. Read the prospectus (a document the company prepares when it's issuing new stocks), and study the balance sheet, which has detailed financial information. (A magnifying glass will probably help you with the fine print.) Then use your instincts to decide if everything you've seen indicates a green light. Here are some tools to help you, Sherlock.

- *Hoover's Handbook of American Business* is published annually and profiles 750 U.S. businesses. It includes company histories, officers, headquarters addresses and phone numbers, sales figures, income, markets, stock prices, products, affiliates and subsidiaries, key competitors, and rankings. For more information contact Hoover's at 1033 La Posada Drive, Suite 250, Austin, TX 78752, (800) 486-8666.

- In addition to general stock market trends, *The Value Line Investment Survey* lists about 1,700 companies by industry. *Value Line* provides projections for financial earnings, revenues, and dividends and ranks the stock on a scale of one to five. This is an excellent place to check out any potential investments.

How to Read an Annual Report

The annual report provides clues to the financial health of a company. Here is a list of the major items that can be found in a typical report and what they mean.

• President's Letter. This is the first place stockholders look for a summary of the company's financial highlights of the last year and an explanation of why profits were up or down. The letter also gives an assessment of the long-term picture.

• Income Statement or Earnings Report. Summarizes the last year's sales volume, other income, and profits or losses, while providing comparative figures for the previous year. The initial figure is the company's net income or net profit; that should be compared with profits over the previous five or ten years.

• Retained Earnings Statement. Tells you what share of the company's profits is being returned to stockholders as dividends and what share is being held back. If the proportion going to you in dividends has declined, find out how the extra funds are being invested.

• Ratio of Assets to Liabilities. Tells you how much of a financial cushion your company would have left if it paid off all its current debts. Large corporations should hold twice as many assets as liabilities.

• Debt-to-Equity Ratio, or Leverage Factor. A measure of the amount of long-term debt your company is carrying in relation to stockholders' investment. The ratio is figured by adding total stockholders' equity. For manufacturing companies, this figure usually is over 50 percent.

• Footnotes. These can provide revealing information. Don't skip them. You may find, for instance, that an exceptionally large profit came from a onetime windfall and probably will not be that high again next year.

- Another good place to look is *Standard & Poor's Stock Reports,* available in large public libraries. It comes out quarterly with weekly updates and contains information on 6,300 companies, including history, earnings, dividends, stock prices, and other financial statistics for the past ten years. An expanded version is also available on CD-ROM. Updated every other week, an annual subscription rate of $995 will supply you with all the information of the print edition, plus consensus opinions of stock analysts for each company and industry information on competing companies.

- The prospectus will give you an idea of what the company does and what it plans to do with the money it raises from the sale of its stock; a balance sheet, which will give you an idea of the assets and liabilities; and a profit and loss statement, which tells the company's income story. You can get all of these from your broker or by contacting the company directly.

After looking at all the evidence, if you still feel the company is looking good, contact your broker and give the go-ahead.

How Am I Doing?

If you want to find out how your stocks are doing on a given day, check the financial section of your local newspaper or one of the major newspapers, like *The New York Times* or *The Wall Street Journal, Standard & Poor's Stock Report,* and *The Value Line Investment Survey.* Most online services like America Online and CompuServe also provide up-to-date information. If your stock isn't listed, chances are that it isn't very popular or widely held.

Beginners often find the stock tables as difficult to decipher as ancient Greek. But with a crash course in translation, most people catch on quickly.

High	Low	Stocks	Div.	Sales in 100s	High	Low	Close	Net CHG.
56	50	McDonalds	1.50	70	55	53	55	+1 1/4

- *High and low, first reference.* Indicates the highest and lowest prices per share for the year.

- *Stocks.* Shows the name of the company, which often is abbreviated. If it is followed by the letters "pf," that indicates it is a preferred stock. "Cv.pf" means it is a convertible preferred stock.

- *Div.* Stands for dividend. This figure shows the annual dividend for one share of this stock is $1.50. This is not a hard-and-fast figure, however. It is only an estimate based on past performance.

- *Sales in 100s.* Tells the number of shares traded that day, expressed in hundreds. In this case, "70" shows that 7,000 shares of McDonald's stock was traded on that day. A "z" preceeding an entry shows the actual number of shares traded.

- *High and low, second reference.* Indicates the highest and lowest price paid for the stock during that day's trading session was $55 and $53.

- *Close.* Shows that the stock was worth $55 at the end of that day.

- *Net CHG.* Indicates that the closing price is $1.25 more than the closing price of the previous day.

Bonds

When you buy a bond from a corporation or a government entity, you are lending money to the issuer, and you become one of its creditors. This is unlike a stock that entitles you to part ownership in a company. Under a bond arrangement, the borrower promises to pay you a specified amount of interest at regular, specified dates, and then to repay the principal on the maturity date, which is printed on the bond. If you purchased a $1,000 bond paying 9 percent interest in semi-annual installments, you could expect to be paid $45 every six months, and at maturity you could expect to receive the $1,000 face value of the bond.

There is an interesting relationship between market interest rates and bond prices. When market interest rates go up, bond prices go down. This is because the value of existing bonds is being determined by a lower rate than the new market interest rate. If you are holding a bond that is earning 3 percent interest and the current interest rate goes up to 5 percent, you are now holding a bond below the interest rate level. You can hold on to it until it matures and still redeem it at its full value. But if you want to sell it, you will sell it at a loss.

Bonds come with different types of interest rates and can be considered short- or long-term investments. A variable interest rate means the rate of interest being paid can rise or fall during a designated period of time. This is riskier than a fixed interest payment, which stays the same throughout the period of the investment, because you cannot be absolutely sure how much interest you will earn in the long run. Variable interest can wind up paying you less than a fixed rate; however, it also can pay more if it rises. The market price of variable interest bonds also tends to be much more stable than that of fixed interest bonds.

Short-term bonds mature in a few months or years; some long-term issues mature after five or ten years, but it could be as many as 30 years from the date of issue. Usually, long-term bonds have higher yields. One reason is that a distant maturity date makes it difficult to predict how financially healthy the borrower will be at the time the bonds fall due. This uncertainty makes it necessary to offer some bonds at higher yields. In addition, investors may expect interest rates to rise, and so they are unwilling to buy long-term bonds with low yields. To attract investors, issuers must offer higher rates.

Financial planners often advise investors to purchase longer-term securities if they think interest rates are high and likely to fall, and short-term securities if they think interest rates are likely to rise. The reason is that if the interest rate drops after you invest in a long-term security with a fixed rate of interest, you are able to reap the benefits of the higher rate of that bond you hold. For example, you have just purchased a fixed rate bond that is paying 8 percent interest; three days from now, the interest rate drops to 7.5 percent. You will continue to earn 8 percent interest on your investment, while anyone who purchases a bond now will have to be satisfied with the lower rate. This means your investment earned money and you didn't have to lift a finger.

Why Buy a Bond?

People purchase bonds for a variety of reasons. They may be seeking a steady cash flow, which the interest provides, and may not have an immediate need for the prin-

Rating Bonds

Standard & Poor's and Moody's are two companies that rate bonds to help investors make the best choice based on their personal tolerance for risk. They employ financial analysts to review the issuer's creditworthiness at the time of the sale of the investment and periodically afterward. The letter rating assigned indicates their assessment of the investment's quality.

S&P	Moody's	What It Means
AAA	Aaa	Your best bet. The issuer's ability to repay the principal is extremely strong.
AA	Aa	High quality. Ability to repay is very strong.
A	A	High-medium quality. Ability to repay is strong although the issuer may be somewhat affected by a difficult economy.
BBB	Baa	Medium quality. Difficult economy may impair the issuer's ability to pay.
BB	Ba	Below investment grade. Ratings below this level become increasingly risky and subject to default.
CCC	Caa	Very risky. Issuer may be about to default, or principal or interest is in jeopardy.
CC	Ca	Highly speculative, and a major risk.
C	C	Lowest rating. Don't expect repayment.
D	D	In default.

cipal. Or they may be looking for a way to diversify their portfolio and fund short- or mid-range goals.

For example, if you want to save to buy a vacation home in five years, you know that if you invest in a bond, you are guaranteed that the principal you invested will be available at the maturity date along with the earned interest.

Another allure of so-called municipal bonds, issued by cities and states and other government entities, is their tax-free status. Most municipal investments are exempt from federal income taxes, and sometimes state and local taxes, too. Because federal income taxes can take up to one-third of your investment income, and state and local taxes are piled on top of that, municipal bonds can seem like a port in a storm.

Invest in bonds if you are looking for a relatively safe investment that will pay you a higher rate of return than a savings account, not if you are looking for a windfall. Most importantly, make sure you are happy with the interest rate of the bond when you purchase it because the market interest rate may rise over time, but your money will be locked up and you won't be able to get at it without suffering a penalty.

There are risks to bond investing, however. There is a danger that the issuer could default. Companies can default when they declare bankruptcy or go out of business, and if that happens, it's impossible for them to honor their debt obligations like your bond. This is particularly dangerous if you have invested in a long-term bond. No one can guarantee what the economy will be like a decade from now, and even big companies that seem like they'll be around forever sometimes fall victim to difficult economic times. Always keep the degree of risk in mind when you're investing in these types of securities, and be prepared with a cushion of "mad" money stashed away, just in case.

Before investing in any bond, check out the reliability of the issuer. Moody's and Standard & Poor's are firms that rate bonds according to several criteria, including the issuer's creditworthiness and the ability to repay the loan (see chart). To reduce your risk, buy bonds that are rated A or above, and select a maturity date that is five years or less.

Types of Bonds

- *Corporate bonds.* Issued by businesses, these bonds come in a variety of forms. In general, though, they can be categorized as secured or unsecured. If the company goes belly-up, investors with secured bonds will be paid first; if there's any money left over, people holding unsecured bonds will then be paid.

- *U.S. government bonds.* U.S. Treasury notes and bonds are considered to be among the safest type of investments. If the government can't pay on its obligations, we're all in pretty big trouble. But because they are so safe, T notes and bonds have a lower yield.

Treasury notes mature in two to ten years. Those with two to three year maturity dates can be purchased for a minimum of $5,000; those with longer maturity dates have a $1,000 minimum. Treasury bonds mature in 10 to 30 years and are available for a minimum investment of $1,000. Interest on the notes and bonds is paid twice a year and is taxable by the federal government (which is paying you money only to take some of it back again), but not state or local governments. An exception to this is Puerto Rican municipal bonds, which are free of both federal and state income taxes.

- *Municipals.* These are issued by state and local governments to fund a variety of projects. Unlike federal government bonds, municipal bonds are subject to default for a variety of reasons. Due to the long-term nature (20 or 30 years) of most municipal bonds, sometimes cities have less income than they planned due to overall economic conditions or just plain bad management. Other reasons these bonds default are that the municipality either spends too much or doesn't raise taxes enough to cover its expenses, which plunges the community into a budget deficit. To put it bluntly, if the bond defaults, you lose all your money, so be extra careful when considering municipal bonds.

In August 1983, the Washington Public Power Supply System (WPPS), known as Whoops, defaulted on $2.25 billion of municipal bonds issued to finance two nuclear power plants. This was the largest municipal bond default in U.S. history, but there have been others. Orange County, California, defaulted on $600 million worth of municipal

bonds in 1994; from 1985 to 1990, 41 municipal bonds representing $500 million defaulted in Colorado; and New York City came very close to the brink in the 1970s. Before investing in a municipal bond, it's a good idea to check its rating with Moody's or Standard & Poor's.

- *Mortgage-backed securities*. Banks and savings and loan associations pool their mortgage loans, then sell portions to investors, who in turn receive payments of principal and interest as the loans are paid off. The risk of default is small; however, sometimes the investment is "prepaid," or paid off before the due date. When this happens, the investor receives all the principal but gets short-changed on the interest that would have been paid if the investment had been allowed to run its course.

Mutual Funds

Mutual fund mania is sweeping the land. For middle America, owning a mutual fund has become as essential as having a big-screen TV and a minivan. The numbers tell the story: There are now more than 6,000 different mutual funds, and one in four U.S. households invests in mutual funds. In the decade between 1984 and 1994, fund assets increased 600 percent from $370 billion in 1984 to $2.2 trillion in 1994. According to a January 12, 1997, *New York Times* article, "the percentage of household assets invested in mutual funds has tripled since 1985." And this figure continues to increase by $20 billion a month.

What Is a Mutual Fund?

A mutual fund is a collection of securities that is managed by a professional financial manager. They allow investors to pool their money together to buy stocks or other investments such as bonds or money market instruments, like CDs, Treasury bills, or short-term loans. When you buy into a mutual fund, you become automatically diversified and you hire an investment pro to watch over your investment's performance. Each fund manager takes the money you invest and buys securities based on the fund's stated financial objectives.

You make money investing in mutual funds exactly the same way you do with individual stocks: through dividends and capital gains. When the mutual fund receives dividends from the individual securities that make up the fund, these dividends are distributed to shareholders. As with stocks, dividends aren't guaranteed, and you are much more likely to make the big bucks through the appreciation of capital gains. You can either receive capital gains by selling off your shares in a mutual fund for more than you purchased them for, or you can receive capital gains distributions from the fund when it sells off some of the securities in its portfolio for a profit.

You can invest in mutual funds through a broker or directly with a mutual fund company that offers them. It's not as crucial to go through a broker to buy mutual funds as it is if you are delving into individual stocks. But if you are a novice to the market, it's probably a good idea to consult an expert first.

Americans have embraced mutual funds for a variety of reasons:

- *Someone else does the work.* You don't have to know a lot of down-and-dirty details about the stock market or investing to make money with a mutual fund. The fund hires full-time professional managers to oversee investments and make the day-to-day decisions about what to buy and sell.

- *They allow you to diversify.* A mutual fund portfolio could include a dozen or a hundred different stocks, bonds, and other investments, of which you are buying a piece. Investing in anything carries with it a certain degree of unpredictability and risk, but if you invest in a mutual fund, it reduces the risk of losing money on one or two bad investments. If the prices of a small percentage of those individual investments in the entire portfolio decline, the effect on the fund's overall performance is minimal. If the value of most of the investments in the fund is still increasing, so is your investment. If you were investing in individual stocks outside a mutual fund and wanted to diversify enough to minimize your risk, you'd need $100,000 to invest in a variety of instruments. Mutual funds allow you to diversify without huge outlays of cash.

- *You don't need big bucks.* You don't have to be Bill Gates to get into a mutual fund and do well. Most funds require an initial investment of $500 to

$3,000, which is within the reach of most middle-income Americans. Many funds now allow you to set up an automatic investment program whereby the company takes the money directly out of your checking or savings account. You can often get started for as little as $50 a month.

- *They're everywhere.* It's easy to find information about mutual funds and sign up. You can invest through a financial planner, a stockbroker, or through a bank. You can even invest directly with a mutual fund yourself. You can call a mutual fund company directly to order a free prospectus discussing the fund's investments and performance. That's a good place to start.

Choosing a mutual fund company is similar to finding a broker in that you can talk to other investors to see who they recommend, look at the ads in *The Wall Street Journal, Barron's, Money, Kiplinger's,* and *Investor's Business Daily,* the business sections of major metropolitan newspapers such as *The New York Times,* and business magazines such as *Forbes, Inc.,* and *Fortune. BusinessWeek* publishes a quarterly and a more comprehensive annual mutual fund scoreboard, both of which rate the performance of the individual funds by category.

MUTUAL FUND PROSPECTUS

It may seem like a drag and it may look confusing, but always read the mutual fund's prospectus before investing. Look for:

- **Investment objectives.** Describes whether the fund's primary focus is for growth or current income and outlines its investments

- **Fund investments.** Discusses the kinds of stocks and bonds it buys. This information should allow you to research the quality of the investments being made

- **Investment risk.** Reveals important statistics that show how volatile the fund has been over a given period: how much it has paid out in dividends, how much was earned from trading securities, and the change in a share's purchase price

- **Summary of fees and expenses.** High fees to managers and other expenses can turn what seems like a potentially good investment into one that's just so-so

Morningstar Mutual Funds is a biweekly publication which tracks over 1,500 mutual funds. It includes a history of each fund's performance, information on the management, ranking against other funds, top holdings, quarterly returns, an analysis of each fund, and risk and returns ratings. For subscription information, contact Morningstar at 225 W. Wacker Drive, Chicago, IL 60606, (800) 735-0700. You can also get to Morningstar's screen on America Online to search for a particular company in which you are interested. You can get a description of the fund, including the investment objective, performance figures, risk measurement, and management details.

Other good sources are:

- *BusinessWeek's Annual Guide to Mutual Funds,* by Jeff Laderman.

- *BusinessWeek* also does an annual mutual fund scoreboard, which rates the performance of the individual funds by category.

- *Mutual Fund Survey* published annually by *Forbes*. For more information, contact the magazine at 62 Fifth Ave., New York, NY 10011. Or call (212) 620-2200.

- *Directory of Mutual Funds,* which lists almost 6,000 funds by category, available from the Investment Company Institute for $8.50. To order the directory, call the Institute at (202) 326-5800, or contact them by mail at 1401 H St. NW, Suite 1200, Washington, DC 20005.

- *Standard & Poor's Directory of Security Dealers in North America,* available in most public libraries or from Standard & Poor's, 65 Broadway, New York, New York 10006, (800) 221-5277. It lists all kinds of broker/dealers, including those that sell mutual funds.

Mutual Funds Are Risky, Too

There is no "perfect" investment, and just like anything else, mutual funds have their risks. Inflation, fluctuations in interest rates and the stock market, and poor management of the fund are some of the factors that can cause investors to lose money. If the stock market as a whole is unhealthy, it means that the value of most stocks is doing poorly. A mutual fund made up mostly of stocks will not be immune and its value will decline, too.

Performance varies from fund to fund, but over the long term, mutual funds can do as well or better than the stock market. In the short term, however, their performances can be poor, so as with any other investment, have realistic expectations and look before you leap.

The key to diversifying mutual funds is to make sure you aren't duplicating your efforts by investing in multiple funds with the same financial objectives. Mix it up between aggressive, growth, value, balanced, and foreign funds. If you find yourself in two or more growth funds, pick the one that's doing better over time and go with it. You also want to have at least one foreign fund in your portfolio because foreign markets don't usually react in sync with the U.S. market. So, if the U.S. market is on the decline, chances are that you will have at least one fund that isn't being affected.

The Lowdown on Loads and Fees

There are a few different types of fees typically associated with the purchase of mutual funds. "Load" refers to the sales commission you pay when the mutual fund company invests your money. Some funds charge the commission when you enter the fund, while others get you when you sell off your shares. The commission is deducted from the original amount of your investment. Loads can be as high as 8.5 percent, but the average is 4 to 6 percent of the investment. A low-load fund is one that charges a commission of 2 to 4 percent of the orignial investment. A no-load fund—a species that has become increasingly popular—charges no sales commission.

12b-1 fees are fees charged against your fund earnings to cover marketing fees, while annual expense fees are charged to cover operating expenses. All funds charge annual expense fees, while only some charge the 12b-1s. Similar to paying common charges on a condominium you might own, you will be charged fees to help pay for the fund manager and her staff of analysts, among other costs associated with running a fund. 12b-1 fees cover the cost of running that full-page mutual fund ad in *Kiplinger's*, trying to attract more investors. You don't actually cut a check to the fund for these fees. Rather, they get deducted directly from the fund's earnings, which in turn may cut into the distributions you receive. Annual expense fees can run as low as .25 percent of the amount of money you have invested in the fund, and as high as 3 percent. Any more than that is excessive and you should reevaluate your presence in the fund.

Types of Mutual Funds

There is a wide array of mutual funds, each with its own goals. Some aim for a high yield now; others want long-term growth. Some carry higher degrees of risk, but offer more opportunity for income. Here are some of the main categories and a brief description of each:

- *Aggressive growth.* These funds invest in new companies that seem promising or old companies that have seen better days, but may be ready for a recovery. They are thought of as high-risk and full of volatility, but if you can stay in them for the long term (at least ten years is advised) to ride out the ups and downs, they're worth the risk. The theory is that the higher returns will compensate you for the higher risk factor, but there are no guarantees.

- *Asset allocation.* Asset allocation is a system of investing that takes into account the theory that different types of assets react to different market conditions. For example, stock prices will rise when interest rates are low, but interest rates don't affect precious metals much. Inflation usually boosts the value of real estate holdings, but the stock market doesn't perform well during times of inflation. By diversifying among a broad spectrum of types of securities—different kinds of stocks, bonds with a variety of maturity dates, real estate, international stocks, various precious metals—you spread your risk the furthest.

- *Balanced funds.* Balanced funds invest in both stocks and bonds with the idea that the diversity of investments protects you from losing too much in any one area. The split is usually 60 percent in common stocks, and 40 percent in bonds and preferred stocks. These provide you with modest growth but lower risk. They won't give you dramatic returns, but they are safer than more volatile stocks.

- *Bond funds*. There are three different categories of bond funds: corporate, U.S. government and government mortgage, and municipal. You can buy short-term (average maturity of one to five years), intermediate-term (average maturity of five to ten years), and long-term (average maturity of 15, 20, or 30 years or longer) funds in each of the categories.

  1. *Corporate bond funds*. These funds invest in companies that are looking to raise cash by issuing bonds. They offer a higher return than government bonds and are slightly more risky. They are for investors looking for a steady monthly income. Although you pay federal taxes on this income, in many areas it is free from state and municipal government taxes.

  2. *Government bond funds*. These funds invest in U.S. Treasury bills (short-term obligations with maturity dates of one year or less); notes (medium-term obligations that mature in one to ten years); and bonds (long-term obligations with maturity dates of ten years or more). They also invest in federally insured mortgages and student loans. With these funds, your principal is pretty much risk-free since it's protected by the "full faith and credit of the U.S. government," but you do have to worry about changing interest rates. When you invest in mutual fund Treasury securities, you need a lower minimum initial investment than if you invest directly, and you can increase your investment whenever you want to in whatever increments are comfortable for you. For example, direct purchases of Treasury bills require a minimum initial investment of $10,000. With a mutual fund, the minimum investment could be a low as $1,000.

  3. *Municipal bond funds*. Although the yields on these bonds are relatively low, their greatest advantage is that any dividend income you receive is free from federal taxes. Some are free from state and local taxes, too. They are ideal for investors in the top tax bracket. Keep in mind, how-

ever, that capital gains distributions are not tax-sheltered and if you are retired, interest from municipal bonds must be included in your total income to calculate how much of your Social Security benefits are taxable. Municipal bonds are rated by Moody's and Standard and Poor's. Consequently, they are relatively low-risk, depending on the investment decisions of the fund's manager.

- *Equity income*. More conservative and less fickle than aggressive growth funds, equity income funds invest in stocks of typically large established companies with records of high, stable dividends. These are more interested in dividends than they are in capital gains and are good for investors who want regular income with some growth potential. Because they are considered low-risk, the rate of return will be reliable, but not spectacular.

- *Gold and precious metals*. These funds invest in stocks of gold-mining firms and other companies involved with precious metals. They once were viewed as a hedge against inflation, but their performance in recent years has brought that into question. They are good for diversification since their performance doesn't follow that of the stock markets, and equity funds don't have any investments in gold. They are less risky than aggressive growth, but more risky than balanced funds.

- *Growth and income*. A growth-and-income fund has a split personality. It invests in well-established stocks, some of which are for capital gains and some for dividend income. Since it runs a course right down the middle of the road between risk and stability, this fund is recommended for everybody. Its reliability makes it great for retirement investing and other long-term objectives, such as college funds.

- *Growth*. These invest more aggressively than balanced funds, with the emphasis on capital gains rather than dividend income. They invest in companies that are not brand-new but are still growing and show potential. Since they're on the riskier side of the investment fence, they're good for long-term investors who can weather the storms and will not need to scramble when the going gets rough.

- *Income.* A variation of equity-income funds, income funds invest in a mixture of stocks, bonds, and money market instruments that will offer the investor dividend income. They are less risky than the overall stock market with returns that are dependable but not sensational.

- *Index.* These funds invest in securities that make up the various indexes such as Standard & Poor's 500, which measures the performance of 500 representative stocks from a wide range of markets and company sizes, or the Russell 2000, which tracks only small-capitalization companies. There are also index funds that invest in gold, utilities, bonds, and foreign stocks. The performance of mutual fund managers is often rated against the performance of the stock indexes. If they do better than the indexes, they're heroes. But the fact is that very few of them beat the indexes.

- *International.* These funds mostly invest in the stocks of companies in foreign countries and should be part of a well-balanced portfolio.

- *Money market funds.* If you are concerned more about safety than making a lot of money, this is the investment for you. Money markets, considered the least risky of all mutual funds, invest in short-term securities such as certificates of deposit and U.S. Treasury bills. However, the increases of these funds are based only on the interest rate and are only somewhat more lucrative than a bank savings account. Financial experts recommend them only as a temporary holding area for money that will be dispersed to more lucrative investments.

- *Mortgage-backed.* These funds invest in Ginnie Maes (Government National Mortgage Association, or GNMAs), a pool of mortgages that the U.S. government has bought from lenders to resell to investors, and ARMs (adjustable-rate mortgages). Although Ginnie Maes are somewhat riskier than bond funds, they offer higher returns, and there is little danger that they will default or miss interest payments since they're backed by the U.S. government. Their major problem is that when interest rates fall, homeowners rush to refinance mortgages at the lower rates, and the Ginnie Mae fund also has to reinvest that money in new mortgages at lower rates. ARMs, with their adjustable rates, don't face that risk since there's no reason for homeowners to refinance when the rates go down, as their mortgage rates will drop, too. ARMs usually have lower yields than Ginnie Maes in compensation for their lower risk. Mortgage-backed funds are good for investors who are looking for steady income-producers and who are not afraid of slightly greater risk than bond funds.

- *Real estate*. These are designed to encourage small investors to participate in a variety of real estate ventures by investing in Real Estate Investment Trusts (REITs). REITs invest in mortgages and commercial real estate. Although real estate hasn't been a stellar performer in the recent past, it's making a comeback. According to a December 30, 1996, *BusinessWeek* article, REITs are predicted to have a 12 to 15 percent total annual return over the next three to five years in markets like suburban and industrial office space. If you get in on the ground floor now, you have the potential for major growth.

- *Sector*. These investments are concentrated in a single industry, like health care, biotechnology, or telecommunications. They're great if the industry is flourishing, but watch out if it takes a dive. They are somewhat risky in that you're concentrating your investment on one area of the market. They are good for long-term investors who can afford possible losses.

- *Small company*. Also known as small-cap, or small-capitalization funds, these funds invest in small companies not necessarily listed on the stock exchanges. Because their performance doesn't follow the stock markets, they're excellent diversification tools. Since they're small, they have the potential for rapid growth and high returns, but they are riskier investments due to their unpredictability.

- *Socially reponsible funds*. They invest in companies that "make a statement" about social responsibility and try to promote a better society. Some funds invest in companies that follow environmentally-conscious practices or are committed to promoting world peace. The risk level here is directly related to the competency of the fund's management. There are socially responsible companies that are terrific investments—and some of these funds have outperformed the market—but a company with a social consciousness doesn't guarantee investors a rate of return. These funds are good for people who are looking for an investment-oriented way to express their support for progressive corporate policies.

Do Your Homework

Before investing in a mutual fund, shop around, review the prospectus carefully, and consider a few key points.

- *How has the fund performed over the past one, three, five, and ten years?* Examining how the fund performed only in one year is not long enough to give an accurate picture. Note how the fund averages out over the long haul. One high-return year may mask a couple of below-average, or even loss, years. Study the performance year by year to determine the fund's true performance.

- *How does this fund compare with others in its category?* You'll need a benchmark of comparison, so look at what other funds like it have done in the same period. Any fund that performs consistently better than its peers is a good bet.

- *How risky is this fund?* Factors to look for: the risk of the fund compared with all other funds; the risk of the fund compared to others in its category; how much the fund's return has fluctuated over time; and how sensitive the fund is to changes in the stock market.

- *Was the current portfolio manager on board during the time periods when the fund was doing well?* Will a new fund manager live up to that same performance?

Investing in stocks, bonds, and mutual funds is like giving your money a vitamin shot. The same amount of money grows and adds health to your savings. But remember, these investments are not without risk and you need to have enough financial resources set aside to compensate for any losses that you may experience. So weigh the pros and cons, set those priorities again, and make your choices. If you decide you just don't have the temperament or desire to deal with the volatility factor, or if you think you're going to be miserable agonizing over every rise and fall, don't go down that street. Find a variety of other investments that will maximize your savings, and relax. But if you decide to take advantage of the opportunities that stocks, bonds, and mutual funds have to offer, it could mean a terrific boost to your savings.

Once you've gotten started on the route to saving big money using the combination of savings accounts and investments in stocks, bonds, and mutual funds, you can apply some strategies to save on the major expenses you'll be making in your life. The next few chapters will show you some valuable techniques you can use whether you're buying life insurance, paying taxes, or buying a house.

THE *truth* about *life* INSURANCE

You're young and fit and getting your life in order. You're even starting a savings and investment program. Now for some life insurance. Leaving it out of the picture is like trying to drive a car with only three tires. It's an essential element in your family's financial stability, now and in the future.

If you're a couple raising children, a single parent, or a couple with one partner who is not able to work, life insurance is something you cannot afford to ignore. Think of it as a safety net that can help you and and your family get through any unforeseen and unfortunate developments that might pop up to jeopardize your lifetime investment strategy.

With 1,600 insurance companies offering more than 40,000 different life insurance policies, sorting out which one is the right match for you is not simple. It's all too easy to commit yourself to a regular schedule of premium payments for a policy that might not be suitable to your needs, but sounded good at the time. You might even be persauded to buy something that you don't really understand.

Instead of being passively led along by an insurance agent who "sells" you on a policy, it makes more sense in the long run to take a little bit of time and effort to educate yourself about the whole business. This chapter is the place to get the details you need to make an informed and intelligent decision about what to get.

What Life Insurance Can Do

The purpose of life insurance is to provide your family with a financial cushion—a so-called instant estate—when you die. There are a number of advantages that life insurance offers your survivors. First, death payments from life insurance, unlike returns from other assets, in most cases are not subject to federal income tax, so the money your family receives will not be whittled away. Nor will they have to wait months or years to receive the proceeds, as they might with other types of investments, because insurance money usually will be available to them shortly after your death. In addition, the amount of money a life insurance policy will provide is guaranteed, unlike other investments, such as stocks, the value of which fluctuates.

Some types of life insurance also provide a way for a family to save money for future use, almost like a savings account, in addition to ensuring death benefits. If you have real difficulty squeezing extra cash from your paycheck to put into a savings account, or if you find it difficult to stick to a savings plan, this may be a route for you to consider, especially if you'll need a nest egg for big-ticket items like your children's college tuition. Life insurance also can help pay off a mortgage or credit card debt, or help provide care for an elderly parent or disabled child if you die in an untimely manner. When those insurance premiums come due, you will be forced to pay—and to save, at the same time. Some policies also guarantee to pay you a lump sum or a specific income for life when you retire.

Another advantage is that should you get into serious financial trouble and creditors storm the barricades to get their share of your assets, they will have much more trouble obtaining funds from your life insurance policy than other investments because of the way the law is written.

While life insurance is an important investment for many people, it is not a substitute for other investment arrangements, which will increase more rapidly and be more valuable. And some people simply do not need life insurance; they should concentrate on investing their money in other ways.

You may decide not to buy life insurance if:

- You are childless and have no dependent relatives;

- You already have substantial savings in other safe assets that will pay you a far bigger return in dividends than a life insurance policy could provide;

- Your spouse is able to work and earn an income he or she could live on;

- Your company has promised to pay you a healthy pension when you retire and include benefits for your spouse if you die;

- You are beyond the age of having to support a family or pay off large expenses.

How Much Do You Need?

If you determine that life insurance should be a brick in your financial foundation, the next step is to figure out how much you need. Obviously, insurance sales reps working on commission are going to convince you that you need a lot. They're very persuasive and their arguments make us weaken in droves. Americans spend more than $6.5 billion a year on life insurance premiums. But the Consumer Federation of America's Insurance Group, a nonprofit group based in Washington, D.C., says about 10 percent of what is spent is unnecessary.

Your best "policy" for buying the proper type and amount of life insurance is to do a little homework before you meet with a sales agent. A family of four should have coverage of at least four to five times the main breadwinner's income; some planners advise having seven or eight times the yearly salary. Therefore, if you earn $50,000 a year, your life insurance policy should be worth a minimum of $200,000 or up to $400,000.

Before buying a policy, consider how much your family would need for living expenses should you meet your Maker tomorrow. Add all of the financial resources you would be leaving your survivors, including savings accounts, money market accounts, stocks, bonds, retirement accounts, mutual funds, and assets that could be sold, such as real estate. If you have a sizable cushion already, you may choose not to buy life insurance. But if there is a gap between what will be needed and what you've already got, use life insurance to cover the difference.

Other factors to consider before purchasing an individual life insurance policy include:

- Will your spouse be generating income after your death, and what would it be, approximately? Would it be enough to live on or would there need to be the kind of supplement life insurance could provide?

- Would your spouse be able to pay off expenses related to your death, such as medical bills and the funeral costs, with the funds that are available?

- Do you have a mortgage on your home? Your insurance could be used to pay off the balance and ensure that your family won't have to sell the house to survive.

- How much will your children need for their college education? College costs today average $10,000 a year at public institutions and up to $20,000 or more at private schools. Enough money has to be available to cover the expense, unless your child will be eligible for grants, student loans, or a scholarship.

- What other large debts are outstanding? Personal loans, auto loans, payments on boats or vacation homes should be factored into the decision with the idea that life insurance will help pay off those debts.

Paying the Price

If life insurance coverage is something you need, check out these ways to cut costs:

• Don't smoke. Smokers may pay almost twice as much as nonsmokers for insurance premiums. Kick the habit—you'll save some money and get healthier at the same time.

• Buy insurance through a club, association, union, or professional organization. Group rates are almost always less expensive.

• Drop some of your life insurance if your children are grown and can support themselves, if your spouse has become financially independent, or if you have a nest egg and no sizable debts.

• Pay insurance premiums annually instead of monthly or quarterly. You'll save on the service charge that is tacked on to each bill.

• Buy from one company and earn a discount. Some companies reduce costs to customers who purchase all of their insurance coverage, including disability, automobile, or homeowner's, from them.

• If you were categorized as high risk because of your job but you have recently switched careers to something safer, let your insurance carrier know so you can be reclassified to a less expensive category.

• Steer clear of agents who try to hard-sell you. Keep in mind that they make five to ten times as much commission selling you a $100,000 cash value policy as a term policy for the same amount.

• Only buy riders, or additions, to your policy that you truly need. Look at them as you would options on a car—expensive luxuries.

• Always, always, always comparison shop. For example, some companies offer term insurance to nonsmokers for 60 cents per $1,000 of coverage, while others charge as much as $4.

- Do you have a group insurance policy where you work? If so, how much will that bring and how much would an individual policy need to supplement that?

Who Can't Get Insurance?

Until the mid-1970s, millions of Americans were denied life insurance coverage as a matter of course, especially people with dangerous occupations, such as wild animal trainers, steeplechase riders, race car drivers, deep sea divers, test pilots, submariners, and miners. Today, thanks to improvements in job safety and court rulings, even armored car drivers and nuclear power plant workers are considered standard risks.

But before agreeing to cover an individual, insurance companies look at several factors. One is your overall health. If you're someone with chronically high blood pressure or an inherited kidney disease, you may be denied coverage outright or, after a medical exam, you will be granted coverage but only at exorbitant rates. People suffering from serious disease, such as AIDS or cancer, may not be able to get coverage at all.

Age is another factor that is considered. If you are 45 or older, you may be required by the insurance company to take a physical exam. As your age increases, so do insurance premiums. By the time you're 70, it's almost impossible to obtain, but by then, few people need it anyway; they no longer have a large family to support, and their retirement income is established.

Gender also is a criterion in setting rates. Unless your insurance company has unisex rates, men will pay more because they have a shorter life expectancy than women.

People who indulge in risky hobbies such as skydiving, rock climbing, and scuba diving are charged extra for premiums. So, too, are those who abuse drugs and alcohol or smoke. In fact, smokers pay up to 50 percent more for life insurance than nonsmokers.

A chart provided by the Consumer Federation of America's Insurance Group shows that a female nonsmoker between the ages of 18 and 30 will pay an average of 68 cents per $1,000 of insurance coverage annually; a male nonsmoker of the same age will pay an average of 76 cents. A female smoker in the same age group will pay $1.01 for the same coverage, and a male smoker will pay $1.05.

Tempting as it may be, don't fudge about bad habits on your life insurance application. The urine specimen you provide during your physical exam will tell the tale. It is tested for nicotine, in addition to other chemicals. If you don't tell the truth about smoking and then die of a smoking-related disease, the insurance company could reduce your survivors' benefits.

Types of Insurance Policies

There are literally thousands of types of insurance policies out there, but no matter what the subspecies, they all descend from a few primary types. Use this as a general guide before turning your attention to the particulars of specific policies.

The main categories of life insurance policies are:

- *Term insurance*. The simplest and least expensive type of policy, term insurance offer protection only for a specific term or period of time. Term policies provide death benefits only and do not build a cash value. If you stop making payment, the coverage will lapse after a grace period. The shorter the period of coverage and the younger you are, the less you'll pay. By contrast, the older you are, the more you will pay, even though your need for life insurance decreases as you age.

BUY DIRECT

If you buy life insurance directly from an insurance company, you can avoid paying a commission to an agent. Two companies that sell policies this way are Ameritas, (800) 552-3553 and USAA, (800) 531-8000. If you've done your homework and are pretty sure you know what you need, this could be a good deal.

An advantage of term insurance, which is favored by many financial experts, is that its cost is reasonable when you are young; if you're in your mid-30s, you can purchase a $500,000 term policy for $850 to $1,500 a year, depending on the insurance company; if you go through a no-load, or no-commission, company, the cost may only be $300 a year. And you can drop the policy whenever you want.

But there are several disadvantages, as well. Premiums on term policies climb as you age, and when the policy expires you must find new insurance. If the policyholder doesn't die during the term the insurance is in effect, the money spent on premiums is essentially wasted and could have been invested in more profitable ways.

The convertible term policy is a cousin of term insurance. It gives you the option of trading your current policy for one that offers permanent protection at a higher premium but does not require that you take another medical exam.

A decreasing term policy provides more coverage earlier in the policy and declines in coverage over time until the policy finally expires. Younger people find these policies attractive because coverage is greatest during the period of their life when expenses and family obligations are heaviest. Since you generally have less need for life insurance in your later years, the fact that the policy ends during your mature years is not seen as a problem.

- *Whole life.* This is also referred to as "straight life" or "ordinary" life; some agents refer to it as a "bank account in an insurance policy" because it increases in cash value over the years, unlike the term policy. By the time the policyholder reaches 65, the cash value often is more than half the face value of the policy.

The advantages of whole life are that you can borrow against the cash value at any time, and the premiums provide shaky savers with an enforced mechanism to build funds for the future. If you stop making payments on the policy, you can choose to be covered in full for a designated period of time or for a reduced amount of the policy's face value for the rest of your life. You also can opt to receive a cash settlement either in a lump sum or in the form of income for a limited period of time.

One major drawback of whole life is that, because of the cash reserve, premiums can be as much as three times higher than term policies. For $350 a year, you might get only $20,000 worth of coverage. In addition, because death benefits are "fixed," whole life policies cannot be altered to reflect the changing needs in your life. Even worse, whole life insurance rewards agents with heavy commissions—commissions extracted from your investment. On a $500,000 term policy, the commission might be as low as $200. In a whole life policy, however, the commission could equal $3,500. Little wonder that agents push whole life policies so zealously.

Some consumer organizations advise against cash value policies, claiming that Individual Retirement Accounts and 401(k) plans are better investments, overall. Still, others point out that cash value policies can pay off if you commit to them for 15 or 20 years, in order to recoup the large up-front costs.

A variation of whole life is called the limited payment life policy in which you pay premiums only for a specific number of years—usually 10, 20, or 30, or until you reach 60 or 65 years of age. Because the premium payments are limited by time, premiums for this type of policy are higher than for a regular whole life policy, but the cash value grows more quickly, too.

Another subspecies is the adjustable life policy. This plan allows the policyholder to change both the premium payments and the face amount of the policy as needs arise and incomes fluctuate.

- *Universal life*. Introduced in the late 1970s, universal life is particularly appealing to those living through the upheaval of the 1990s. Many younger people favor universal life for its flexibility, a characteristic that is not present in most standard whole life policies. It allows you to vary the amount of coverage and the amount of the premium payments, which is a particularly nice feature if your income fluctuates. It also offers greater flexibility than other types of insurance in allowing policyholders to draw from the policy's cash value.

A whole life policy is something like a short-term investment instrument because the cash value of the policy is separated from the insurance aspect, with the money earning variable interest. But if you're thinking of investing in universal life policies rather than mutual funds or other investment products, think again. Their returns, of about 4 percent, just don't stack up, and your overall return is eaten away by company fees and agent commissions.

- *Variable life*. This option is appealing to people who want the assurance of standard insurance benefits as well as the ability to have more hands-on control of the cash value portion of their policy, at least to some extent. Policyholders can direct the company to invest the cash in low-risk, low-yield securities such as relatively safe stocks, bonds, mutual funds, or money market accounts. And, like other cash value policies, the returns are not taxed until the money is withdrawn from the policy.

Of course, this ability to invest the cash value also increases the risk involved. The amount of the cash reserve can fluctuate or be severely reduced, depending on the performance of the investments. Another drawback is that variable life insurance is expensive because of hefty sales commissions and service fees. A return of 10 percent could be reduced to 7 or 8 percent over 15 years because of these fees.

- *Single-premium life insurance.* This is another alternative for someone who wants to invest and earn tax-deferred returns as well as death benefits. Policyholders pay a onetime substantial lump sum, a premium of $5,000 or more, and the cash value portion of the policy is invested. Policyholders can access the cash through loans, but penalties are imposed if the policy is canceled within a few years of purchase. The emphasis, financial planners say, is on the investment aspect of the policy, rather than on the insurance.

So, What Should I Buy?

Everyone's individual situation is different, but here are some thoughts on what type of life insurance coverage you might want to consider before purchasing:

- *If you're solo.* You've graduated from college and you're just starting out, you have no dependent family members, you don't plan to marry, and you have enough money to cover death-related expenses. Hold off on buying any life insurance.

- *If your funds are limited.* Buy term insurance that is renewable and convertible. Later, when you can afford pricier premiums, you can explore the pros and cons of converting if you choose to.

- *If saving for retirement seems impossible.* Purchase a policy that provides a cushy retirement income, with limited life insurance protection in the meantime.

- *If you are a disciplined saver capable of building a healthy nest egg.* Buy a straight life policy that offers a death benefit just covering immediate cash needs and death-related expenses.

- *If you are 40 or over.* Start off with straight life for your long-term needs. But don't go for this higher-priced policy if it means blowing your budget and skimping on your regular savings and investment program. Instead, consider buying a term insurance policy for a fraction of that premium amount and putting the difference into a savings account or other investment instrument.

Children and their future needs are an important determining factor when shopping for insurance coverage. If you have no children and both spouses are working and earning enough income to be self-supporting, you may not need to have an individual life insurance policy that provides death benefits.

Jordan and Mindy are a married, dual-income couple in their late 20s. Jordan's job as a reporter at a mid-sized metropolitan newspaper pays him $28,000 a year, while Mindy earns about $19,000 as a copywriter at a small advertising agency. Because Jordan's employer provides a modest life insurance policy, and because both partners are capable of earning a living should the other die, they have decided to hold off on purchasing life insurance. Some insurance experts, however, would advise the couple to invest in a $20,000 straight life insurance policy with an option permitting them to buy more insurance later, up to a certain amount, without having to undergo a

LIFE INSURANCE FROM BANKS

Savings banks offer limited, low-cost term and cash value insurance to residents of New York, Connecticut, and Massachusetts, and because it's sold directly, you avoid the sales commissions you would pay if you bought it through an insurance company or agent.

Policies are available from both state-administered Savings Bank Life Insurance (SBLI) and private companies. Some commercial banks in those states have recently started selling life insurance, too.

If you live in one of those parts of the country and are not looking for a fancy policy, it might be worth checking out.

medical examination. The relatively small initial cost of the premiums would give them the ability to increase their coverage as their family needs grow and, at the same time, it would provide a growing financial reserve in the form of the cash value.

Unlike Jordan and Mindy, people with children have less of a choice about whether or not to invest in life insurance: They should, without a doubt. Young families need to be concerned about having immediate protection should the primary breadwinner die. Their best bet is to buy life insurance as early as they can and purchase a type that will give the most protection now, even if the policy will expire later.

STRING SAVER #16

Keep your home's heating equipment well maintained and have furnaces serviced annually. If you live in a cool climate, insulate your outlet covers and check for leaks in windows and doors. Ask your utility company if it offers a free tour of your home to suggest energy-saving tips.

Ken and Jeannine are both 31 years old, married, and have two daughters, six and nine years old. Jeannine stays home with the girls while Ken provides the family's $53,000-a-year income working as a physician's assistant. He has a group policy that would pay a year's income as well as a $20,000 straight life policy bought before the birth of their first daughter. The couple's primary need is for immediate protection that would provide income for Jeannine in case of Ken's death, while the children are dependent, and would later pay for their college education. They also would like to build some form of nest egg for emergencies.

To achieve these goals, the couple should consider buying a $50,000 straight life policy with a 20-year family income provision, or rider, which would provide a monthly income for Jeannine for two decades. That, along with benefits from his group policy and Social Security death benefits, would provide enough monthly income for the family to get by.

Don't Need It, Don't Buy It

The insurance industry is endlessly creative in devising new ways for consumers to spend their money. One way to decide whether or not you need a new insurance product is to stay focused on the real purpose of insurance: to protect you against catastrophic losses that you couldn't handle yourself by tapping into your own resources. Another way is to ask yourself if the insurance coverage is so narrow—airplane crash insurance, for example—that the money you spend insuring against such an unlikely event isn't worth the benefits your survivors would receive.

Consumer organizations and financial planners agree that you should save your money and pass on these policies:

- *Life insurance for children.* When a baby arrives, the parents are bombarded by insurance agents trying to sell them life insurance for their offspring. The sales pitch comes complete with a song and dance about how the insurance can provide a college fund through an increase in cash value. But there are far better investments to provide a college fund than life insurance. Remember: The purpose of insurance is to protect against the loss of a family member's income. Unless you are the parents of a child star, forget this policy.

- *Credit life insurance.* The pitch often arrives in the mail, amid an array of fliers. The advertisement, often from a credit card company, a finance company, or a car dealership, claims that if you purchase this policy, payments will be made should you die or become disabled. There are a few problems: First, the premiums are usually outrageously expensive and—read the fine print—the deal is that the insurer will only pay the minimum on your balance, often for not more than a year. Meanwhile, interest continues to build and the balance grows. Rather than buying this type of policy, channel more funds into your emergency savings stash.

- *Mortgage protection insurance.* This is similar to credit life because the insurer promises to make your mortgage payments for six to 12 months in the event of disability or death. Again, the same drawbacks exist. The length payments are made is limited and the policy is quite expensive, up to 4 percent of your annual mortgage payment.

- *Dread-disease insurance.* These policies cover you in case you get a particular disease, such as cancer. These are poor bets because the payout is typically just 50 cents or less on each premium dollar. Instead, invest in a policy that covers all diseases, if your employer doesn't already provide health insurance.

- *Flight insurance.* The cost is high, and no matter how afraid you are of flying, chances are you won't die on that flight from Boise to Buffalo. Statistics show that you are 56 times more likely to be killed in a car accident than a plane crash. So save your money.

Where to Get It

No matter where you ultimately purchase the policy, shop around first. Similar insurance policies can vary wildly in price. There are three primary sources of life insurance coverage:

1. *Your employer.* Many companies pay all or part of the premiums on life insurance policies for their employees. This is a great deal, but be sure to check exactly what the coverage includes. If necessary, supplement it with an individual policy.

2. *Low-load insurance companies.* It is possible to purchase insurance directly from some insurance companies without going through an insurance agent. This can save a substantial amount paid on sales commission. For a list of low-load companies, contact your state insurance commission or:

   Consumer Federation of America's Insurance Group
   414 A St., SE
   Washington, DC 20003
   (202) 547-6426

American Council of Life Insurance
1001 Pennsylvania Ave., NW
Washington, DC 20004
(202) 624-2000

Shop around by calling different companies and asking for information on various policies and prices.

3. *Insurance agents.* Like auto mechanics, insurance agents generate a great deal of public skepticism, especially because they work mainly on commission. The way to find a good one is by asking friends, relatives, and coworkers for a recommendation. Reputable agents can explain the pros and cons of different policies and help select the one that best suits your needs. They can direct you to companies that will accept you even if you are a high risk because of a medical or occupational issue. They also can follow up with you every few years to discuss new policies if your needs have changed.

Look for an agent who represents one or more of the top companies with a proven record of stability, as rated by Standard & Poor's or an insurance rating firm called A. M. Best, which has been publishing annual reports about insurance companies since 1905. Preferably, the agent should be someone who is a chartered life underwriter or a chartered financial consultant. It's not a foolproof method of determining honesty and quality, but it shows the agent met the credentials of the rating firms.

But just as in any profession, there are dishonest characters around, so approach with caution. Be very skeptical of computer-produced charts packed with glowing information about future projections. In most cases, they don't happen. Falling interest rates have made it difficult for companies to meet their promised projections, although some unscrupulous sorts continue to make sales based on this false information. In some cases, policyholders were told they would earn a certain amount within eight to ten years and, in fact, it will take up to 20 years to match the projections.

Also, watch out for agents who try to sell you a policy that does not suit your needs because it guarantees them a higher commission, and those who urge you to exchange one cash value policy for another. You may benefit if the new policy offers a better rate of return, but in most cases, if you examine the fine print closely, you're better off sticking with the policy you've got. That is because little, if any, cash value is accumulated within the first two years of a policy when heavy fees and commissions are being paid. This practice of exchanging a new policy for a perfectly good one is called twisting, and it is illegal.

STRING SAVER #17

Have health insurance coverage, if at all possible. Your life savings and everything you've worked so hard for can disappear very quickly in the event of a major illness. New federal legislation will help ease the health insurance dilemma by allowing workers to carry over health insurance from one job to another, even if there is a preexisting condition. If your job doesn't offer health insurance, try joining one of the group plans offered by professional organizations, chambers of commerce, and other such groups.

A Word about Disability Insurance

So far, all of the discussion has focused on life insurance and its shadowy companion, death. But death may not be the only bad thing that happens to you. In fact, you are seven times more likely to become disabled before you retire than die. Disability, physical or mental, can rob you of your capacity to work and generate income. The effects of disability wreak havoc with your family's immediate financial picture. But, unlike the expenses associated with death, the costs linked to disability can continue to mount for many years. Without proper planning, your family may never recover its financial balance.

As part of your long-term financial strategy, be sure to investigate disability insurance policies as well as life insurance coverage. A general guideline is that the amount of coverage you will be paid by the policy should equal 60 to 70 percent of your gross earned income. In many cases, the disability income will be tax-free, which can go a long way to making up the difference.

If your company does not provide disability coverage, you will want to search for your own to give yourself some peace of mind that, should the worst happen, you won't be without income. As with anything else, shop around before you buy. There are two general types of disability insurance: "any" occupation coverage and "own" occupation coverage.

Any occupation coverage will take effect only if your disability prevents you from working at any job, even scrubbing toilets at a rest stop or flipping burgers. This means, of course, that you would be left to scrounge along on wages you could barely survive on.

Own occupation coverage takes effect if your disability prevents you from working at your profession. For example, a teacher with a head injury would have a difficult time functioning in the classroom.

Neither policy takes effect for several months after the onset of the disability, a time span known as an elimination period. The elimination period can range from one month to one year. The longer the elimination period you agree to, the less expensive the premiums. Be sure you have enough money on hand to provide for your expenses during the elimination period.

A Word about Annuities

Many people are confused about annuities because they are sold by life insurance companies. But annuities are not life insurance. Unlike life insurance, which provides your survivors with an income if you die, an annuity provides you with a retirement income that will supplement your Social Security and pension checks.

An annuity is a contract in which the insurance company accepts a sum of money from you and, in

STRING SAVER #18

Buy items like socks and stockings in bulk. If you lose a sock or get a run in one leg, you'll have a match and be able to prolong the life of the item. Socks, stockings, and underwear often are less expensive when they come in a package of three or five.

RATING INSURANCE COMPANIES

It's important to choose an insurance company that is financially sound and not likely to go out of business before you die. If this happens, you've been paying premiums for absolutely nothing. Check your company's rating with one of these major insurance raters:

A. M. Best
Ambest Rd.
Old Wick, NJ 08858
(800) 424-BEST

Duff & Phelps
55 E. Monroe St.
Chicago, IL 60603
(312) 368-3198

Moody's
99 Church St.
New York, NY 10007
(212) 553-0377

Standard & Poor's
25 Broadway
New York, NY 10004
(212) 208-1527

Weiss Ratings
P.O. Box 109665
Palm Beach
Gardens, FL 33410
(800) 289-9222

turn, guarantees to pay you a monthly income in your later years. The size of your payments are based on your life expectancy and how much money you put in up front. Women, who tend to live longer, receive smaller payments than men, although they are spread out over a longer period of time.

Some people favor annuities because they are blanket guarantees that free you from some of the devils of retirement planning and provide assurance that you will never outlive your income. But an annuity should never be your sole source of retirement income. While you're still young, invest in stocks and other instruments that will generate more.

GET *ahold* of your TAXES

CHAPTER SIX

Nobody likes paying taxes— you might even be the kind of person who approaches the whole subject with what therapists call an "attitude of denial." It's time to admit it. You're a grown-up now, and knowing a little bit about taxes is something grown-ups do. Relax. It will make you seem worldly and wise.

Learning about taxes is an important step in laying the foundation for a solid financial future. Believe it or not, paying taxes correctly—meaning that you take all of the deductions available to you—is one way to save money. Why pay more than you have to? Pay attention to taxes and take advantage of the ways you can save money on your returns. If you know how the game is played, you could end up saving lots of money—money you could spend on fun things like a cappuccino machine or a kayak. Or, you could take the extra cash that you would otherwise have forked over to a faceless, soulless bureaucracy, invest it, and make even more money.

Imagine that you're a kid who's been given an allowance; then, Mommy and Daddy come to you and say they want some of it back. Of course, you'll stomp your little feet and cry, "No!" Then you'll devise ingenious ways to repay as little as possible. Income taxes operate on the same principle. Let us help you with your strategy. Rest assured— this isn't going to be one of those dreary, complicated lectures that only accounting wonks fathom. These are simple, understandable steps you can take to reduce the amount of money you have to pay Uncle Sam.

Can You Say "Tax Bracket"?

The amount of federal, state, and local taxes you pay is determined by how much money you make. The IRS places you into one of several categories, called tax brackets, accordingly. Knowing your tax bracket is important because it tells you what percent of your gross income you'll actually get to keep.

Currently there are five brackets: 15 percent, 28 percent, 31 percent, 36 percent, and 39.6 percent. Theoretically, the more money you make, the higher your tax bracket. But by claiming as many deductions as possible, you can reduce the tax rate you pay. To determine your tax bracket, get your hands on a copy of the latest IRS rate schedules, available from a professional tax preparer or your local IRS office. Even though the federal taxes take the biggest bite, don't forget to calculate state and local taxes into the equation to get a truer picture of the amount of taxes you're paying.

Educate Yourself

Knowledge is power, so spend some time learning a bit about tax laws and preparation. You don't need to immerse yourself. Taxes are complex—it takes experts years to learn all about the ins and outs, and the rules are constantly changing. But there are a number of free or low-cost pamphlets published by the Internal Revenue Service that provide helpful, basic information on topics such as your rights as a taxpayer, tax

information for homeowners, self-employment taxes, and free tax services. Contact your local IRS office for more information about obtaining them.

Start Your Preparation Early

Taxes are easier to deal with when you have a plan. If you keep a flurry of receipts and records tucked everywhere, getting your taxes done on time will end up taking on the high-anxiety frenzy of cramming for a huge final exam. Why would you put yourself through this? Don't get stressed—get organized. Buy a small filing cabinet just for storing tax-related information: current receipts, past and present copies of tax forms, and documentation that will help you prove your deductible expenses. Keep a notebook where you can jot down deductions as they occur, such as mileage for business trips (the IRS allows you to deduct 30 cents per mile, or operating expenses, for the vehicle). And you may want to check out some software that can help you organize and calculate your tax expenses. (The resources section on page 195 has some suggestions.)

Getting organized will do more than calm your nerves; it will save you lots of time and energy hunting for the records you need. It saves you money, too. Remember that $50 pledge you made to the local public television station in May? Chances are, if you don't keep organized records, you won't think about it the following April when you're doing your taxes—and donations are tax-deductible. Forgetting your donations and losing the deduction is like throwing your money away.

Find a Good Tax Preparer

If figuring out your taxes is a relatively simple matter that doesn't involve a lot of itemized deductions, you may want to file the tax forms yourself. But if you don't feel confident about completing the forms, or simply don't want to take the time, you'll need to find a good tax preparer. Don't wait until March to start the search; begin in September or October when the April 15 deadline isn't looming. Avoid choosing a tax preparer based solely on an advertisement. Get referrals from friends, business partners, or professionals who are handling your other investments, then do some interviewing before you make a final decision.

Not only will a good tax preparer save you time and give you the security of knowing that your taxes are done correctly, but a competent professional can save you money by maneuvering you through the tax law maze to find the most favorable payment scenario. Did you know that the cellular telephone you use for work is tax-deductible? Did you know that the points on your home mortgage are deductible? How about the fees you paid to that employment agency last year when you were hunting for a new job? Or those childbirth classes you took? Even the cost of the tax preparation itself? Your tax preparer knows—that knowledge will save you cash and maybe even set you up for a refund.

Make Contributions to Your IRA or Keogh Plan Early in the Year

Tax deniers who wait until April 15 to claim IRA or Keogh deductions for the previous year wind up losing a nice chunk of compounded interest. If you contribute $2,000 to your IRA at 9 percent interest every January 1, in 30 years you'll have $297,150. If you wait until April 15 of the following year to invest it—just squeezing in under the wire—you'll have $264,098. You'll have lost $33,052—enough to make a sizable down payment on a house, buy a car, or fund a couple of years of your child's college education.

Make Yourself Disaster-Proof

Take an inventory of your possessions, or make photos or a videotape of them in case disaster strikes. Keep a record of these purchases in a special place with your tax materials. If you're burglarized, you will be able to deduct the loss. You also can deduct property loss in the event of a flood, fire, tornado, hurricane, sonic boom, vandalism, storms, and automobile accidents.

Use the Long Form

Married taxpayers have a choice of using the long form 1040, or the short form 1040A. Use the long form so that you can itemize deductions and get more of a tax break. This is essential if your taxable income is $50,000 or more.

Customize Your Deductions

Learning all about tax deductions can be an overwhelming and time-consuming task. Instead, target your efforts, and learn as much about tax breaks in your profession as possible. Get advice from a tax professional and ask colleagues in your field for tips. Patrick, a new international sales rep for a toy manufacturer, was overjoyed when he learned that the sales tax he paid on business-related items during a recent trip to Canada for a toy convention were tax-deductible in the United States.

Readjust Your Withholding

If you are overpaying the government, talk to your employer about readjusting the amount of federal or state income tax that is being withheld from your paycheck. You'll know this is happening if you usually get a hefty refund check. Refunds are pleasant surprises, of course, but they mean that the government has been hanging on to your money when you could have been using it to invest. After you readjust your withholding, don't spend the extra cash. Invest it in your tax-deferred IRA and reap the long-term rewards.

Don't Pay Taxes on Income That Isn't Taxable

Professional tax preparers are aware of what income isn't taxable. But if you're doing your own forms, make sure you've got all the details before you send the money to Uncle Sam; you may wind up paying more than you have to. Among the types of income you don't have to report are gifts, inheritances, life insurance proceeds, child support payments, personal injury damages, disability benefits, refundable rental security deposits, rebates on new cars, and utility company rebates for buying energy-saving devices.

Put Off Paying Taxes as Long as Possible

Sock as much money as you can into tax-deferred investments such as IRAs, municipal bonds, savings bonds, annuities, and Treasury bills. Buying and holding on to stock and real estate are other ways to own assets that appreciate, but do not require you to pay taxes on the appreciated value until it is sold. The tax that is paid when these types of investments are sold is called a capital gains tax. Avoid it for as long as you can.

The best way to avoid that nasty capital gains tax is to do what wealthy Americans do: Hold on to your assets and avoid selling them for as long as possible. Many rich people have most of their assets in real estate or stocks that have appreciated in value from one generation to the next.

WHAT YOU'LL OWE

Taxable Income	Tax Rate
Married Couples Filing Jointly	
$0 to $40,000	15%
$40,001 to $96,900	28%
$96,901 to $147,700	31%
$147,701 to $263,750	36%
Over $263,750	39.6%
Singles	
$0 to $24,000	15%
$24,001 to $58,150	28%
$58,151 to $121,300	31%
$121,301 to $263,750	36%
Over $263,750	39.6%

Real estate and stocks can skyrocket in value over the years and you don't have to pay a penny to the government as long as they remain in your possession. But the minute you sell them, you're going to be paying a hefty capital gains tax.

If you must sell your home, for example, you can avoid paying the capital gains tax if you purchase another home of equal or greater value within two years. If the new home is less expensive, however, you will be held responsible for some taxes.

Be Charitable by December 31

Donations of clothing, furniture, and used books can be deducted; so can the number of miles you drive back and forth to the hospital where you work as a volunteer. Do as much charitable giving as you can by the end of the year and deduct it.

Don't Pay a Penalty

If you underpay your income taxes, the IRS attaches a penalty, sometimes hundreds of dollars. Avoid that bit of nasty business by making sure you are paying at least as much in taxes as last year or more, especially if your income has risen. If you aren't, and you think you'll end up owing money, this is the time to ask your employer to increase the amount of taxes withheld from your salary.

Be Smart If You're Going It Alone

If you choose not to work with a professional tax preparer but instead venture into the jungle of tax preparation alone, be sure that you are well armed. Before you plan to fill out your forms, bone up on some of the guides and directories that are available at bookstores and libraries. To make the job easier, you may choose to buy user-friendly tax preparation software programs such as Turbo Tax, MacInTax, and ProSeries, from Intuit; TaxCut from Kiplinger's; and Proper™ Personal Financial Planning Software from Ernst & Young. These programs cost from $25 to $50 and can be purchased directly from the manufacturers or through a local retailer. The programs usually check for inconsistencies or incomplete items, which could catch the eye of the IRS; they also cut down on mathematical errors. If you run into snags, free assistance is available from the IRS, which has created a network of telephone tax consultants and audiotapes. Often, around the tax season, local universities also offer free tax preparation help to residents of the area. And don't forget the Internet as a source of information.

STRING SAVER #19

Make the purchase of a used car contingent on the car getting a clean bill of health from an auto mechanic you trust.

Here are three Web sites to keep in mind:

- L.A. Professionals Online (http://www.primenet.com/laig/proserve). This site provides generic information from attorneys, certified public accountants, and medical professionals. It offers a bulletin section about tax issues, including an analysis of IRS guidelines for independent contractors.

- TaxSITES (http://www.best.com/ftmexpat/html/taxsites.html). This site also provides tax-related information and contains links to several sites, including tax forms, frequently asked questions, tax laws, and tax software.

- United States Tax Code Online (http://www.fourmilab.ch/ustax/ustax.html). This site provides interactive access to the complete text of the Internal Revenue Code.

Consider Filing Electronically

You can file your taxes the old-fashioned way, by "snail mail," or, like more than 12 million other taxpayers, you can file electronically, because the IRS has finally come online and become, by its own definition, "service oriented." Filing electronically creates a quicker turnaround time for refunds, generally a few weeks. If you want to file electronically, contact a local preparer; many of them are set up to do this. Income tax preparation software also allows you to automatically file electronically. You should be aware, though, that you have to pay for the privilege of this greater service orientation. It can cost $30 or more to file electronically.

The "A" Word

Audit. It sends a chill down every taxpayer's spine. Each year, over one million tax returns are audited. Although that sounds like a lot, that represents less than 1 percent of all returns. Audits are nothing to be afraid of if you have been honest and forthright in submitting your tax forms, and if you have kept good records of your income and expenses. It is important to understand that, while it may seem tempting to fudge on your income tax forms, it could land you in serious trouble. There are plenty of ways that you, with the help of a good tax preparer, can cut your tax bill without resorting to falsehoods and misrepresentations.

There are a few reasons why you might be audited:

- Reporting an income of over $50,000

- Claiming a significantly higher number and amount of deductions than you did on last year's return

- Having mathematical errors on your return

- Claiming deductions for a home office

There are five types of audits:

1. *Taxpayer Compliance Management Program.* This program kicks into gear every three years and is designed to scrutinize, line by line, the tax forms

of about 100,000 people. Don't think you're safe just because you've received a refund or a year has passed since you filed the return. The IRS can audit a return up to three years after it has been filed.

2. *Mail audits.* If there is a minor problem, such as a math error or a deduction that is not allowable, it's usually handled by mail. You may only have to complete some forms or submit copies of receipts to resolve the problem.

3. *Field audits.* These are generally targeted to businesses. An IRS agent handling the case will notify you of suspected problems, then arrange a time to visit your home or business to review your records. This procedure can take one to three days.

4. *Office audits.* The most common type of audit, this informs you that two or three areas in your tax return are under scrutiny. You are asked to bring records relating to that information to the local IRS office where they can be examined. The trickiest areas include child care, automobile and entertainment expenses, cash contributions to organizations, and losses from natural disasters. Make sure you keep good records on these items.

5. *Criminal audits.* If the IRS suspects you of criminal fraud, you're in deep water. This type of audit could result in severe penalties or a jail sentence. If you're going to be criminally audited, get a lawyer. If you have been honest on your tax returns, you have little to worry about, although four out of five of those who are audited do end up paying something. Only a small percentage pay nothing or get an unexpected refund. During your meetings with the IRS, follow this advice:

- If the questions are beyond the most basic type, take along your tax preparer.

- Don't volunteer any information that was not specifically asked for. You might open doors to other avenues of questioning. Don't give the auditor the opportunity to go there.

- Remain calm, professional, and polite. Don't vent your spleen in front of the IRS agent. It only makes the situation more tense. Act courteous, matter-of-fact, and look for areas of compromise.

- If you owe and are strapped for the money, work out an installment plan with the IRS.

- Appeal the decision in tax court, if you feel the ruling was unfair. But remember, fighting the IRS is no piece of cake. It takes time and can be quite expensive. But it's to your benefit to come forward and be truthful. The IRS doesn't prosecute people who willingly admit their omissions and take a course of action to correct them.

Tax Preparers

A good professional can save you money, as well as time and energy, by knowing tax laws thoroughly and helping you take advantage of all of the deductions to which you are entitled. Some, particularly certified public accountants, can also represent you if the Internal Revenue Service should come calling.

The type and quality of tax preparers varies widely from sole proprietors who fill out forms at a kitchen table, to chain, or "storefront," preparers, such as H & R Block, who churn the masses through their doors between January and April. There are also highly trained CPAs and enrolled agents (EAs), trained and licensed tax preparers who can represent you before the IRS.

Who you choose to help prepare your taxes depends on what you want. Sole proprietors usually charge the least—$25 to $45—and are best when your tax situation is simple and straightforward. They typically will not represent you during IRS questioning. Keep in mind that "tabletop" tax preparers can be just as qualified as others; it is important to do some background research to be sure you are getting what you pay for.

Millions head for storefront preparers because their rates are relatively inexpensive; expect to pay $50 to $100 for a basic form and about $150 or slightly more if your tax situation is more complex. Some of the preparers work full-time, others work part-time, and their level of expertise varies, although all have been trained by the company. In some cases, storefront preparers have a policy of standing by clients during IRS questioning; others do not.

Interviewing a Tax Preparer

Here are some questions you always want to ask someone before he prepares your taxes:

• What is your experience and training in the field? The more experience the better.

• How much will it cost and how do you calculate that fee? Make sure you get all the numbers up front and that you won't be charged any hidden fees after your taxes are prepared.

• Do you check returns for accuracy? Walk right away from anyone who answers "no" to this question.

• Are you available for questions throughout the year or only during the tax season?

• How often are your clients audited? If the answer is never, the tax preparer probably is being too conservative and the client is not getting all the deductions to which he is entitled. If the answer is more than one in 70 for clients earning less than $50,000, and more than one in 20 for clients earning more than $50,000, there could be a problem with the preparer.

• Will you represent me if I am audited? You want preparers who will stick by their work if you are called before the IRS.

• Have you had any experience dealing with IRS appeals?

• Will you pay any penalties or interest resulting from a tax preparation error? Has this ever happened?

• Can you give me names of some of your current clients to use as references?

Here are the national headquarters of the country's two largest storefront tax preparers. You can contact them for the office nearest you.

H & R Block
4400 Main St.
Kansas City, MO 64111
(800) TAX-7733

Jackson Hewitt
4575 Bonney Rd.
Virginia Beach, VA 23462
(800) 234-1040

If you're more comfortable with a solo practitioner, the Internet has a useful site sponsored by the National Association of Tax Practitioners (NATP), whose members include CPAs, individual practitioners, enrolled agents, accountants, attorneys, and financial planners. You can find tax professionals in your area by visiting NATP's Web site at http://www.natptax.com, and searching a member database organized alphabetically by city. For more information, contact:

STRING SAVER #20

Be willing to pay for a second opinion from a reputable physician. It's a sound medical practice and a good investment that could save you hundreds or thousands of dollars on an unnecessary procedure.

National Association of Tax Practitioners
720 Association Drive
Appleton, WI 54914
(800) 558-3402
(800) 839-0001

CPAs and EAs often have a more select clientele with more complex tax situations, such as business owners or upper-income clients, and their rates—$75 an hour or more—reflect that. If you go to a CPA, expect to pay, on average, $250 to $500 for tax preparation. In addition to filling out tax forms annually, they often serve as year-round financial advisers who offer practical advice about ways to save on taxes next year, unlike tabletop and storefront preparers. If your situation is complicated or you are concerned about an IRS audit, select a good CPA. As always, do your homework before you select a tax preparer, and interview several candidates before making a final choice.

You can find tax preparers by looking in the Yellow Pages of your local directory or contacting the local chamber of commerce. The business department of area colleges and universities, which often sponsor tax preparation assistance for residents of the community, can refer you to qualified tax preparers. Word of mouth works in this situation, too. Talk to colleagues, business associates, and friends in similar fields to get recommendations.

For a list of the members of the American Institute of Certified Public Accountants in your area, call (800) 862-4272. For a list of members of the National Association of Enrolled Agents in your area, call (800) 424-4339.

Online tax preparers include Compucraft (http://www.cctax.com) and Tax Fighters (http://www.av.qnet.com/%7eisiboy/taxfight.htm). Tax Fighters also can be reached by mail at P.O. Box 5036, Lancaster, CA 93539; fax: (805) 722-0418, or e-mail at taxfighter@qnet.com.

You can obtain IRS forms and publications by calling (800) 829-3676.

You can get additional tax information by visiting FedWorld on the Internet at http://www.ustreas.gov/

Did You Know You Can...

- Give "deferred income" gifts, such as low-income securities and U.S. savings bonds, to children under age 14?

- Claim a dependency deduction for children in college for whom you provide over half the support? Children over 24 years old also can be claimed as deductions if their income is below a certain amount.

- Claim a dependency deduction on your parents or other family members for whom you provide more than half of their support?

- Take a deduction if you've donated to charity stock that has appreciated in value, which helps you avoid paying any capital gains tax?

- Take a tax deduction for unneeded clothing or personal items donated to charity? You also can deduct all cash charitable contributions you make and any auto mileage associated with charitable work.

- Get a deduction if you loaned money to someone other than a relative who won't pay you back?

- Deduct most of the cost of a hotel room if a spouse accompanies you on a business trip?

- Deduct the cost of house-hunting expenses incurred by a move related to business?

- File returns separately rather than jointly with your spouse if it means lower taxes? It's unusual, but sometimes married people wind up paying less if they file separate returns.

- Amend your return if you discover you paid too much the previous year? You might wind up with a refund. But don't delay—there is a time limit on amendments.

TAKING *the* home-buying PLUNGE

You're driving around one day when you see it—the house of your dreams. Suddenly, you're in love. And best of all, there's a "For Sale" sign out front! Elated and excited, you feel like rushing to the nearest real estate office so you can lock up the deal before any other suitors come along and whisk away your honey.

But hold your horses, pardner. Get a grip. Buying a house is a major commitment, like marriage. In fact, mortgages last longer than many marriages. Before rushing to the altar, maybe you'll want to play the field a bit, look around at other houses. And you'll certainly need to stop and ask yourself some questions before you buy:

• Is it in my best interest financially to buy a house?

121

- Can I afford this house?

- Will this particular house be a good long-term investment for me?

To Buy or Not to Buy? That Is the Question

If you are now renting, you need to ask yourself whether buying a home is in your best interest. The obvious answer would seem to be "yes." Owning a home has long been touted as one of the best investments that can be made.

Over the past decade, the appreciation of houses has exceeded the rate of inflation by at least one percentage point a year, making home ownership a sound investment. In addition, the longer you stay in a home, the more you build equity, which is the appraised value of the home minus the outstanding balance on the mortgage. In the future, you can use that equity, or value, to get a tax-deductible bank loan to finance other expenses, such as paying for a child's college education. You also can use that equity to provide a loan to cushion your retirement. When you rent, you build up no equity, and there is no investment value in the money you are spending. Unlike other types of debt, the interest you pay on a mortgage is tax deductible and will be a financial benefit when April 15 rolls around.

While home ownership generally is a good investment for most people, there are those who would find it more beneficial to continue renting. If you plan to move within five years, either because of a job transfer or for other reasons, renting is often a better option financially. That is because there are a number of costs related to both buying and selling a home. Homes appreciate slowly, and you may be losing money if you buy and sell within a short period of time.

Renting may also be your best bet if rents in your community are very inexpensive, and you would like low housing costs so that you have the ability to save for other things. It's usually a good idea to rent if the monthly expense would be 65 percent or less than the average mortgage payment in your community. Renters also can skip the seemingly endless parade of expenses attached to maintaining a home. Want the plumbing fixed? Call the landlord.

It's important to remember, though, that rents rise, so don't count on those low rates forever.

Can You Afford to Own a Home?

Here's a bracing statistic: The average cost of a home in small-town America is now $110,000, and residents of metropolitan areas such as New York and Los Angeles can expect to pay twice as much.

But hey. Who thinks of money when they're in love? Very few of us can separate our emotions from our logic when we are strongly attracted to something we want. That is why so many homeowners wind up "house poor."

That's the trap that Gary and Karen fell into. Long-time renters in their early 30s, they were convinced that, with Gary's $35,000-a-year salary as a firefighter, they could handle the $120,000 mortgage on a four-bedroom ranch house in the country, situated on an acre of land. It would be a perfect place to raise their two young children and would give their beloved Labradors room to romp. They were swept away by images of themselves in their new home without carefully calculating how much it would all cost.

One rule of thumb is that the cost of a house should not exceed 2 1/2 times your annual salary. Because Karen and Gary have always been thrifty, they figured they could manage to stretch their budget beyond that, and they convinced an eager real estate agent and a lender that they could, too.

Their initial expenses started slowly; there were just the costs associated with traveling significant distances around the rural Pennsylvania county to see different houses, and paying for lunches out, and babysitters.

STRING SAVER #21

Make a list before you do your grocery shopping. Figure out a weekly menu and buy what you need for that. Organize your list, and eliminate nonfood items, such as toothpaste, that often can be purchased for less at discount chains.

When they found the house they wanted to buy, they were faced with having to make a down payment. Down payments can be as low as 5 percent of the total cost of the house, but most lenders require between 10 and 20 percent. Most experts agree that you should make as large a down payment as you can afford because it cuts down on the total amount of mortgage interest you will pay. Before signing an agreement of sale, insist that the deposit will accrue interest.

In addition to the down payment, there are closing costs—often amounting to about 5 percent of the purchase price—which can add as much as several thousand dollars to the total cost. You need to live in the house at least five years to recoup these costs in appreciation.

Closing costs include:

- *Points.* The most notorious of the closing costs, these are charges made by the lender to compensate them for low-interest mortgages. Each point equals 1 percent of the loan amount. If your mortgage is $168,000, one point would equal $1,680. If your lender is asking you to pay three points, on the $168,000 mortgage that would equal $5,040 more. Look for mortgages with the least amount of points.

- *Escrow account.* Since 1994, the federal government has allowed the mortgage lender to establish an escrow account equal to two months' worth of mortgage payments in case the borrower falls behind on the mortgage or property tax payments. This is the good news. In the past, lenders could require borrowers to make an escrow account deposit equal to six or eight months of mortgage payments.

- *Mortgage application fee.* You are charged about $250 or more, depending on the lender, for processing your application.

- *Origination fee.* The mortgage company charges you about $100 to process your loan.

- *Mortgage insurance fee.* If you cannot swing a 20 percent down payment, the lender may require you to purchase this to insure that the difference between your down payment and the 20 percent can be paid. To avoid this, make at least that 20 percent down payment. Remember, the more you put down, the less you need to borrow and the smaller the mortgage payments and mortgage insurance fee will be.

- *Appraisal fee.* The bank requires that a professional assess the market value of your intended home to make sure that what you intend to pay is a fair price. Of course, you foot the bill for this: about $350 to $500.

- *Home inspection fee.* You pay another professional about $400 to inspect the house for defects in the foundation, the roof, the windows, the plumbing, and environmental safety.

- *Credit report fee.* The bank charges you a fee of about $50 when it runs a check on your credit history.

- *Bank attorney fees.* You are charged for any legal work the bank must have done associated with approval of the mortgage. Expect to pay about $500.

- *Title search fee and insurance.* You are charged for a routine investigation to make sure that the seller has the right to transfer the property to you. The actual cost depends on the amount of your mortgage. Title insurance protects the lender against any problems that might occur in the transfer of records, such as illegal transference or liens.

STRING SAVER #22

Keep lamps, candles, and television sets away from thermostats. They can throw off the room temperature by making the thermostat "think" the room is warmer than it really is.

- *Notary fees.* You are charged about $100 to have all necessary documentation notarized.

If you're strapped for cash, one way to save money is to negotiate with the seller to pick up some of the closing costs, which would normally be paid by you, the buyer.

GET GIFTS EARLY

If relatives are planning to give you money gifts to help with a house down payment, ask them to give you the money several months before you intend to apply for a mortgage. Lenders are less likely to approve a mortgage if the down payment is a gift because they worry that you might not be financially secure enough to make the down payment yourself. If you get the gift early, though, and deposit it into an account months ahead of time, it will appear as a personal asset.

If the seller is eager to unload the property, perhaps because of a new job transfer, you may get lucky.

Gary and Karen weren't that fortunate. After making the down payment and paying for all the closing costs, they were bombarded with expenses they hadn't planned on: moving costs, additional furniture to fill more rooms, property taxes and homeowners insurance, and higher utilities and maintenance than they'd planned. All of a sudden, the bills seemed like an avalanche.

While the couple is going to be able to meet the hefty mortgage for the next 30 years by spending only for necessities, there is precious little left over for extras like investments or vacations. Karen, who always wanted to be a stay-at-home mom, is considering going back to work to bring in extra money for basic expenses.

Lesson? Only fall in love with what you can afford. Before you think about buying, calculate all of your present income and expenses. This should give you a good idea of how much more you can stretch to meet a mortgage and all the other expenses associated with home ownership.

Beware the temptation to press to the upper limits of your budget. Ask yourself how your family would continue meeting the mortgage obligation if one of you lost a job. Rather than squeezing the last penny out of your carefully constructed budget and submitting to the shackles of house poverty, consider buying a house which is a bit less than you can afford, so you will have funds left over for investing and other activities.

This approach proved to be a lifesaver for Oliver and Linda, a two-career couple. They each earned about $38,000 a year and with their combined incomes, the pair could

have bought a much more expensive home than the small Cape Cod they settled on, but they were experts at living beneath their means. When they applied for a mortgage, they based what they could afford only on Oliver's income, choosing not to use any of Linda's earnings for the payment.

When Oliver suddenly lost his job, Linda was easily able to continue paying the mortgage and all of the other household bills until Oliver was re-employed. That would not have happened if they had stretched their budget like a violin string.

New home buyers may want to start out by purchasing a multifamily home in a good neighborhood, which generally is less expensive than a single-family home. Multifamily homes have a history of appreciating in value, too.

Is This House a Good Long-Term Investment?

Wendy, a well-paid director of public relations for a hospital, was smitten with a majestic home in a developing rural area. It had all the features she wanted and more. And she was just a little proud that it was by far the most outstanding home in the neighborhood, which was mainly comprised of modest, prefabricated ranches. She bit.

And she violated basic real estate rule number one: Location is everything.

DEAL WITH A MORTGAGE BROKER

For the best deal on a mortgage, it may be to your advantage to work with a mortgage broker. Because they have access to mortgage databases, they can often come up with loans that are offered at the lowest rates. The lender pays their commission and you're under no obligation to take whatever they find you. Your real estate agent can recommend some mortgage brokers, or you can find their ads in the real estate section of your newspaper.

The area in which you live—how far from an urban area you are and who your neighbors are—has a profound impact on the long-term value of your home. Property owners in one municipality were infuriated when local officials allowed an entrepreneur to open a mushroom farm within a mile of their homes. Not only did the business invite more traffic to their aging roads, but when the wind was right, a pungent aroma emanated from the farm and blanketed the area. Property values dropped like a stone. People who tried to sell their homes found few takers.

Wendy's situation was not that extreme, but the same principle applies. Real estate experts caution against owning the fanciest house in the neighborhood or making extravagant home improvements that outshine everyone else. Pricey homes don't appreciate as much as more humble abodes do. Those wallflower prefabs surrounding Wendy's rose of a house caused some of its glory, and its value, to fade. Better to buy the least expensive house in an upscale neighborhood and make improvements. That way, your house will appreciate more in value.

Wherever you decide to buy, be sure to do a thorough check of the area first. Take a tour of the neighborhood and drive the back streets. One couple, unfamiliar with the town where they were buying a house, knew only one way to get to the property. If they had learned an alternate route and checked it out, they would have discovered that the house was within a quarter-mile of a garbage dump, which was not a great boost for property values. They only learned about the dump after they bought the house and moved in. Suddenly, they understood why they were able to get the property at such a great price.

SELL BEFORE YOU BUY

If you're planning to buy a new home, sell your old one first. Even if you have to temporarily rent quarters before you can move into your **new home,** do that instead of depleting your savings trying to keep up two mortgages.

Couples who are planning to have children or who have children already need to check on the quality of schools in the district. People who commute to work will want to factor in the drive time. They need to decide whether living so far away from an employer would rack up large bills for fuel and auto repairs.

Talk to neighbors and town officials about property taxes. These are taxes you pay annually. Some people make arrangements with the mortgage company to pay them and then they add that to the monthly mortgage payment, so don't forget to figure this amount into your budget. You might be able to get a comparable house in a town with lower property taxes. Sometimes communities with higher property taxes have better schools and more services—trash pickup, recreational facilities, police protection, for example—but that's not always the case. There are communities with a higher percentage of corporate offices or industry that bear the lion's share of the tax burden, which relieves the pressure on homeowners.

To get an overall sense of the community and its desirability as a housing market, walk or drive around town. Are many of the homes falling into disrepair? Are businesses fading? Read the local newspaper and attend a community meeting to find out what issues concern residents. Also, check out crime and vandalism in the neighborhood, the amount of traffic, whether there are vacant homes and buildings nearby, and whether heavy industry operates in the area.

But don't only examine the location of the community before you buy; also consider the neighboring towns. Are the surrounding communities as desirable as the one you're considering? Is the house you're looking at sitting on the border of the town next to a community that's not as attractive? Is the housing market thriving in the region of the country you're considering, or is it depressed, as it generally is in the Northeast?

In addition to location, consider the type of home you are buying when you are house-shopping as a long-term investment. Existing homes that are several years old tend to be less expensive than brand new homes, because they also require more maintenance. You may love that 175-year-old stone farmhouse on six acres of land. But it won't be a good investment if you have to face an endless stream of repairs that keep you forever low on cash.

THINK BEFORE YOU RENOVATE

Some home remodeling projects will allow you to recoup the expense when it's time to sell. Others add little or nothing to the resale value.

Best renovations:
• Bathroom remodeling or the addition of a new bathroom
• The addition of a family room
• An upgrade or addition of a master bedroom suite
• Deck and sunroom additions

Worst renovations:
• Swimming pool
• Tennis court
• Turrets
• Hot tubs
• Customized or built-in furnishings
• Deluxe wall and floor coverings

Negotiating with the Seller

All right, you've done your research. You've decided that owning a home is really for you. You've thought hard about what type of house would be best for your family and calculated how far your budget can stretch to meet the new demands. Through savings and wise investment strategies, you've saved enough for a down payment. You've found a house that looks like it could be The One.

Now it's time to begin negotiating with the seller in order to save yourself some money. Don't be afraid to drive a hard bargain. This probably will be the biggest investment of your life, so don't worry too much about appearing overly nice, and don't let your emotions about the house cloud your judgment.

BUYING VERSUS RENTING

Wonder whether it would be better to rent or buy? **Software** is available to help you make the calculations. One is a program called "Buying Your Home," from Home Equity Software. Another is "Buy or Rent," available from Real Estate Consultants.

First, as always, do your homework. Before you can make a reasonable bid, you need to know whether the sale price is in line with those of other similar homes in that area. Check with a real estate agent, then get a second opinion from other agents, neighbors, or municipal officials. Read the real estate listings in the local paper for several weeks to get a sense of fair housing prices in the area.

Learn as much as you can about the seller. Talk to neighbors and listen to what the seller himself says about his situation. Someone else's misfortune may be your best bargaining tool—and your best bet for saving money. Someone who has just divorced and is in financial straits will be anxious to sell at a good price. So will children who inherited a home they don't want, people who already have bought another house and are strapped with two mortgage payments, and people who are being transferred and need to move quickly. Also anxious to unload are developers who are in financial distress and need to sell quickly to generate revenue, banks that have foreclosed on mortgages but now find the property costly to hold on to, and owners of "oddball" houses, such as a home

created from an old schoolhouse, who are having trouble finding a buyer with eccentric tastes.

Learn as much as you can about the property itself before making an offer. If repairs are needed, factor the cost of that into your offer. If you're handy, you can save thousands of dollars in the final bid by fixing minor problems yourself relatively inexpensively. Things like broken windows, dangling downspouts, old fixtures, and worn rugs don't cost that much to correct. On the other hand, run like the wind from a home that needs costly and complicated repairs. A wet basement, a buckled or cracked foundation, inadequate plumbing, or problems with the septic system are really bad signs.

Another factor to consider is whether the major appliances will be left in the home or if the seller is planning to take them along. Adjust your bid accordingly.

A general rule when bidding on a well-maintained home that is reasonably priced is to begin negotiations 8 to 10 percent below the asking price. Twenty percent below what the owner is asking could be construed as insulting and might be rejected out of hand; 5 percent would not leave much room for haggling.

Getting a Mortgage

Selecting the most suitable mortgage for you can be a mind-boggling experience because there are so many variations. Keep in mind that there are three main types of mortgages: fixed-rate, adjustable rate, and balloon mortgages.

A fixed-rate mortgage is a loan whose rate of interest stays the same until the mortgage is paid off, or amortized, to use banking lingo. These are most desirable when you can lock in at a relatively low interest rate, perhaps 9 percent or less, and when you plan to stay in your home for a number of years. People who like to play it safe often prefer a

STRING SAVER #23

If you shop in so-called warehouse stores, shop carefully. Unless you're very disciplined, you may end up buying merchandise you don't need, thinking you're getting a bargain. Stick closely to your budget and buy only what you can use before it spoils.

fixed rate mortgage because it gives them the security of knowing that no matter how much interest rates fluctuate, their monthly mortgage will stay the same.

BUY FROM THE GOVERNMENT

The Resolution Trust Corporation (RTC) is a government agency that sells off property held by owners who could no longer make the payments, and that could mean a **good deal** for you. A wide variety of houses and apartments is offered. Some are better deals than others because of their location and condition. But with some persistence, you may be able to find the house you've been looking for. Check your phone book for your local RTC office or call (904) 488-4197 for a list of residential properties.

An adjustable rate mortgage (ARM) is a loan whose interest rate, and monthly payments, fluctuates upward or downward once or twice a year over the life of the loan. To prevent payments from going through the roof, however, the ARM does have two "caps," or maximums. There is a cap on how much your mortgage can increase during a specific period of time; there is another on how much it can increase over the life of the loan. Because ARM payments typically start off lower than those of fixed-rate mortgages, they are preferred by people who don't have a lot of money immediately but expect their incomes to increase, and by people who don't plan to stay in the house very long.

With a balloon mortgage, you will make fixed-rate payments for a designated number of years, then pay off the balance in full, which means you will either have to refinance the mortgage or sell the house. Very low rates make this loan attractive, especially to buyers who plan to sell the house before the final payoff is due.

After deciding what type of mortgage to apply for, you will need to select the length of repayment. Mortgages typically are paid off over 15 or 30 years. Financial experts agree that in most cases paying off a mortgage as quickly as possible is the best way to save money over the long haul. Although monthly payments will be higher with a 15-year mortgage, the amount of money saved in interest payments is substantial.

For example, If you take out a $100,000 mortage for 30 years and pay 8 percent interest, your monthly payments will be $733, and you will pay a total of $264,153, including interest, over the life of the loan. If your mortgage is for 15 years, your monthly payments will be $955 and the total, with interest, will be $172,017. Your total savings: $92,136.

Lenders consider several factors in granting a loan:

• Your credit record for the past two or three years

• Your current debt load

• Your personal assets

• Your income

If you have a clean credit record, a steady income, and are not overloaded on credit card, auto, or other debts, you should be able to obtain a mortgage. To find out your credit rating, contact one of the local credit bureaus listed under "Credit Rating Agencies" in your phone book.

It is important to learn about your credit rating and how much of a mortgage you would be eligible for before you start to house-hunt. That will give you some realistic boundaries to work within. If possible, have your potential lender prequalify you for the loan, either informally, through a word-of-mouth agreement, or more formally, with a loan approval letter.

A Word about Real Estate Agents and Buyers' Brokers

In most cases, people buy their house with the help of a real estate agent, someone who is trained

TAPE YOUR TRIPS

It's a good idea to take a notebook and a video camera along when you're looking for a house. Record important information and features of each house. That way, you can review the information at home as many times as you like and won't have to rely on your memory.

and licensed by the state. Agents, also known as brokers, can be very helpful in matching clients with affordable homes in the area of their choice. They also handle paperwork and communicate with the seller. However, it is important to remember that, as pleasant and helpful as they may be, they are working for—and paid a commission by—the seller, not the buyer. Because of this, their perspective is going to be biased.

Agents are required by law to tell buyers any information they want to know about the physical aspects of the house: Does the basement flood, for instance, or has the property tested positive for radon? They do not have to disclose other types of information that may affect the buyer's decision, such as the fact that someone was murdered in the house six months ago or that a huge shopping mall is going to be built across the street next year.

One alternative is to work with a buyer's broker, who only represents the interests of home buyers. Buyer's brokers, who list their services in the Yellow Pages, can help their clients to negotiate the lowest possible price with the seller. They are paid an hourly, flat fee, or a percentage of the sale by the buyer, or they may share in the real estate agent's standard 6 percent commission.

Agree to work with either a real estate agent or a buyer's broker if:

- The broker works full-time at the job and is serious about the profession. Avoid part-time dabblers, who won't work as hard for you.

- The broker has a thriving business. Ask how many homes the agent has listed in the past year. There is no correct number, but if it seems like very few, look elsewhere.

- The broker specializes in the kind of house and neighborhood you are shopping for. If you are looking for a modest "starter" home, you will get scant attention from an agent who specializes in upscale, luxury residences.

- The broker lives in the community. Newcomers probably will not know the market as well as someone who has lived in the area for awhile.

Home Equity Loans

Home equity loans are being heavily marketed to consumers as an easy way to tap into credit to be used for vacations, a second home, gifts, a college education—whatever.

There are many different plans, but essentially a home equity loan allows homeowners to borrow 70 to 80 percent of the appraised value of their house, minus what is owed on it. The length of the loan can last from 5 to 12 years or more, depending on the lender.

How much credit you are allowed depends on your income and your ability to pay. Home equity loans usually have variable interest rates, which are lower than credit card interest rates, making them especially attractive to those who are looking to borrow with the least amount of obligation. However, there is no cap on the rates, so often the interest rates can increase dramatically.

Because they are made to sound so convenient, so warm and fuzzy, it is difficult for some people to remember that what they are really doing is taking out a second mortgage. If they should have trouble repaying the loan, they put their house in jeopardy. A home equity loan should be approached with caution and used only for large and important necessities that cannot be financed any other way.

Retire with the Help of Your Home

For all of those years, you supported your house. When you retire, it may be time for your house to support you. Buying a home can be part of your retirement planning strategy.

Retired people who are cash poor may choose to take out a reverse mortgage to supplement their income. With a regular mortgage, you pay the lender until, at the end of 15 or 30 years, you own the home. With a reverse mortgage, the lender issues the homeowner a loan based on a percent-

KEEP RECORDS

Home improvements, such as adding a room or a deck, can be added to the cost of your home to calculate capital gains. Hold on to every home improvement record to prove the adjusted cost of your home when capital gains taxes are assessed.

age of the equity in the home, usually 20 to 60 percent. Retirees can receive the money as a lump sum or in monthly or quarterly payments.

How much you receive depends on your age, the interest rate, and the value of the property. You receive more if the property is valued highly, interest rates are low, and the length of the loan is short because you are quite elderly. You receive less if the property value is modest, interest rates are high, and you are younger, making it necessary to take out a longer loan.

You shouldn't plan to live off the income from a reverse mortgage because, depending on your circumstances, the payments can be small. However, they are most helpful to people who need income for a short period and then plan to sell their house. One real drawback is that you are essentially selling back your home to the lender. If you outlive the reverse mortgage, you may have to sell your house and move.

TAILOR *your* financial plan *to your* NEEDS

A financial plan is not a document carved in stone. Rather, it is a guide, a road map, that gives you direction. People aren't static creatures. Our life and circumstances change, and every new phase brings its own set of special financial considerations.

View your financial plan as a never-ending work-in-progress, and be prepared to adapt your financial strategy to your circumstances.

Singles

If you are single and have a tough time making ends meet, take comfort in the fact that you are not alone. But the fact that financial planning is especially difficult for singles doesn't excuse you from not trying to build a monetary cushion for yourself. If you're not married, it's even more important for you to have a sizable nest egg, because if you become unemployed or ill, you don't have a second income to fall back on.

At 27, Joy is the youngest elected official in her city, but the honor and attention that brings do not translate into a hefty salary. She gets by on the paycheck of a public servant using several techniques:

STRING SAVER #24

Prepay the principal on your mortgage. An extra $200 to $300 a month can cut a 30-year mortgage down to 15 years and save more than $100,000 in interest.

- She bought a twin home, which is less expensive than most single-family homes, within walking distance of her office. Not only does she pay a reasonable mortgage she can afford, she also has cut down considerably on commuting expenses.

- Joy turned a large basement area with its own bathroom into a studio apartment, which she rents to a female college student, whom she has carefully screened.

- Joy and several other singles in the neighborhood pool their cash and buy food and nonperishable items in bulk at a local discount store, a move that saves all of them money.

- Using food bought in bulk, Joy cooks one large meal, planning for leftovers. Instead of going out to a restaurant, she and her friends take turns hosting each other for simple meals one night a week in their homes.

- She rents movies, attends free or low-cost cultural events and, if she wants to try a snazzy new restaurant, eats a reasonably priced lunch there rather than a more expensive dinner, and she takes home the leftovers.

- When she goes on vacation, Joy cuts the cost of traveling solo by sharing a hotel room or ship's cabin with another single woman.

Dating is an area where singles can be particularly vulnerable, financially as well as emotionally. It's important to remember one thing: Money can't buy true love. So don't succumb to a temptation to shower your current flame with expensive tokens of affection. Small gestures, such as a humorous greeting card, a well-timed phone call, an e-mail message, or a small bouquet of flowers, can be just as endearing. If you split, you'll be relieved that you didn't waste your money on buying that Rolex; if you get married, you'll be glad to have the extra money for your nest egg.

When you date, agree to share the costs—what your parents called "going Dutch"— so neither one of you has to shoulder all of the financial burden. It's okay to splurge once in awhile, but if you see each other regularly, choose low-cost activities, such as going on nature walks. If there is a college or university in your area, check out the activities schedule; they often sponsor free or inexpensive events, such as concerts and lectures.

Singles should not overlook the key areas of buying insurance, investing, and planning for retirement. It's every bit as important for single people to provide for their children's future as it is for couples. If you don't have children, consider others who might depend on you and your financial support, such as aging parents or a younger sibling you are helping send through college. If you're single, disability insurance is particularly important because you don't have a spouse to support you if you cannot work.

Investing and retirement strategies (discussed in chapters six, seven, and eleven) follow the same rules for singles as they do for couples. Financial planners do caution singles not to be overly conservative in their investment strategies for fear of losing money. It is particularly crucial for singles to have a sufficient nest egg to help with larger purchases, such as a house, and to help fund retirement. Aggressive investing is the only way to achieve that.

Mingles

"Mingles," an unmarried couple of the same or different genders living together, have different concerns than married couples, especially in the early part of their relationship. It is unlikely that they will have to worry about joint investing, retirement planning, or insurance coverage. Typically, mingles keep separate checking and savings accounts, and approach long-term planning as if they were going to continue to be single. However, before moving in together the mingled couple does need to sit down and openly discuss their individual earnings and assets, and how those funds will be budgeted.

Some unmarried couples split all of their expenses—rent, phone bill, and so on—right down the middle, each one contributing 50 percent. This works best when both earn comparable salaries. Others assign household expenses, depending on income and personal preferences. One may pay the rent, for example, while another may pay the grocery bill. If there is a major difference in income—one earns $20,000 and the other $60,000—they may chip in amounts proportional to their income. The high earner could pay two-thirds of the rent, for example.

As the relationship builds, you may have property or activities that you want to fund jointly. Tom and Margaret, mingled for two years, decided to buy a car together. They created a special savings account for the car and each added money to it weekly from their separate paychecks. When it came time to make the purchase, the title was put in both their names so they could have joint ownership. If one partner were to die, the other would inherit the property immediately. The same action can be taken if you decide to purchase a house together.

At some point, when you both feel comfortable with the idea, consider having an attorney draw up a contract that clearly designates how property and assets would be divvied up in case of a split, and how outstanding debts would be paid.

Taking the Vow

There are thousands of adjustments people have to make when they marry, but few are as critical as learning how to handle money as a team rather than as independent individuals. Suddenly, you need to consider how your spending and saving patterns affect both of you and your long-term plans together, not just yourself. The first step, even before you walk down the aisle, is to see your union as a financial partnership, as well as a spiritual one.

Just as you wouldn't think of marrying someone without knowing quite a bit about his or her personal habits, you shouldn't marry someone without knowing and accepting his or her financial habits. Many marriage counselors and divorce court officials can attest to the consequences of that oversight.

Talk openly about how much money each of you makes, what credit card and other debts you have, and what your assets are. Figure out how much your joint worth will be and talk about how that would affect buying a house, raising children, and saving for retirement. Discuss how each of you will spend and save money, and work out a comfortable compromise. For example, if one of you uses credit cards liberally and the other sparingly, consider eliminating all but one credit card each. That way, you still can charge, when necessary, but in a more limited way that will prevent you from becoming overloaded with debt. Not discussing the financial aspect of your relationship ahead of time can have disastrous consequences.

Before they were engaged, Frank and Rachel didn't pay much attention to the differences in their spending patterns. Rachel was raised to be a devout saver; she was so thrifty that she even reused the bows from gifts so she wouldn't have to buy new ones. Frank sometimes teased her about being a tightwad, but she just laughed. Frank, on the other hand, believed you can't take it with you. He had a soft spot for expensive audio equipment; every time he got some spare cash, he quickly bought a new item.

A pattern that seemed kind of cute during their courtship turned calamitous after their marriage. Because Frank couldn't seem to stop spending money on unnecessary items, Rachel had to use most of her paycheck to meet the household expenses. And although she had been a saver all her life, she let the habit lapse out of discouragement and frustration. Arguments about money ensued and, before they knew it, Frank and Rachel had more than just money problems to grapple with.

The scenario is typical and highlights the importance of sitting down together before the wedding day to hammer out the details of your financial life. One of the first places to start is with the wedding ceremony itself. The decisions you make about the wedding day can set you on the road to a solid financial future or leave you on shaky ground from the outset.

Unless your parents are paying all of the bills—and even if they are—opt for a smaller wedding rather than a lavish affair, and start a savings account with the extra money. Rather than going on an expensive, three-week trip abroad for your honeymoon, stay closer to home and take a one-week vacation. Agree to save or invest gift money. Down the road, you can use that money to buy a house, or you can simply continue to reinvest and watch it grow.

Before marriage, or as soon afterward as possible, discuss what your short-term, mid-range, and long-term financial goals are. If they differ, look for areas where you can compromise. If, for example, one of you wants to save $1,000 a month and the other finds that excessive and lobbies instead for $500 a month, you could compromise by agreeing to save $750 or $800 a month and increase that amount as your income rises. Promise that when you get raises you will save the money.

Work out a realistic budget by "trying on" different scenarios for saving and spending patterns. Nick and Elaine, a salesman and a schoolteacher, have the good fortune to be financially compatible; both believe that saving and investing are essential to their future. For them, the easiest thing to do was to designate one partner as the "bill payer" and the other as the "saver." While Nick pays all household expenses, including the mortgage, food, credit card bills, automobile expenses, and so forth, Elaine puts her entire paycheck into savings and investment vehicles. Those funds are used to meet short-term goals, such as a two-week vacation at the beach next summer, mid-term goals, such as buying a new car in three or four years, and long-term goals, such as paying for their son's college tuition and padding their retirement nest egg.

Other couples might not find this a workable solution. Some may choose to split the household expenses and have both contribute to a savings account. Couples who like to maintain a degree of independence may keep checking and savings accounts in joint names for their "together" plans and expenses and also keep separate accounts in their own names. This can contribute to a sense of autonomy, but it can become confusing if good record-keeping lapses.

One way to keep track of your expenditures is to create a monthly spending chart, with budgeted amounts at the top of each column. You may agree to allow $200 a month for entertainment expenses. If you go out to eat and spend $53, record that figure on the chart, and you will both know that you have $147 left to spend. However you choose to budget your money, it is essential to work on a plan together and review it periodically to see how it is working and where changes could be made.

Once you have created a budget you both can live with, set aside money to build a contingency, or emergency fund, that will equal at least six months' income. That will be your savings starting point. When you have achieved that and paid off your major debts, except for a mortgage, devise an investment strategy that will help you meet various goals, perhaps with the help of a financial planner. If you come to the marriage with investments, consider joining them into one account to save on maintenance fees paid on separate accounts.

In addition to budgeting and investing, you will need to discuss your insurance needs and retirement plans. (See chapters five and eight.) Assess what you have and what you need. Decide together what types of insurance will suit your needs now, and in the future. Participate in your companies' 401(k) plans or open Individual Retirement Accounts. And don't forget to review your tax filing status. Consult a financial planner or an accountant to determine whether filing jointly or separately would save you money. Call the American Institute of Certified Public Accountants (AICPA) at (212) 596-6200 for a list of these people in your area.

Having Children

Until fairly recently, it was expected that people who married would have children; if they didn't, they were looked upon as selfish or pitiful souls. Today, attitudes are changing, and more couples than ever before are choosing to remain childless, a move which greatly enhances their chances for long-term financial stability and independence.

Despite changing attitudes, though, most married couples still become parents, and the younger they are, the less prepared they are for the expense. The cost of raising just one child takes over $200,000, not including college education. When you have two or more, the expenses really soar.

It all begins before the baby is born. Plan to spend $3,000 for a hospital delivery, and at least $2,000 more on prenatal care, maternity clothing, furniture and clothing for the baby, and other necessities. When the child is born, there are obvious expenses such as food, clothing, medical and educational expenses, and day care. But would-be parents often forget to factor in the "hidden" cost of child-rearing—thousands of dollars in lost income if one parent decides to stay home to raise the child.

Financial planning should begin before a child is born; ideally, before that child is conceived. The first step is for you, as parents-to-be, to check on your health care and medical coverage to see what expenses will be paid by insurance; also find out about your company's maternity leave policy to see what sort of salary you will be receiving, if any, while you are out. When you have a handle on this, create a "baby fund"—a savings account, certificate of deposit, or money market account—into which money will be deposited regularly to take care of as many of the early expenses as possible.

Parents who don't have medical insurance, don't want to pay $3,000 for a hospital delivery, or simply want a more comfortable, homey environment where they can deliver their baby, can turn to less expensive alternatives. Mary Ann and Jack, a couple in their mid-20s, decided to have their daughter at a state-licensed birthing center run by a group of nurse-midwives. Although the center was not attached to a hospital, a doctor was on call 24 hours a day, in case of complications. Mary Ann checked with her doctor before agreeing to delivery at the center, which charged about $2,000—saving the couple $1,000 over the cost of a traditional hospital delivery. They would have saved even more if they had opted for a home delivery attended by a licensed nurse-midwife. The price tag: $800 to $2,000. Birthing centers and nurse-midwives can be located with the help of your local hospital or in the Yellow Pages.

STRING SAVER #25

Close off your fireplace. When it isn't being used, a fireplace lets warm air out and brings cool air in.

When children are born, it is important that you buy life and disability insurance policies to reflect the changing needs of your family and to protect their financial future. (See chapter five.) This also is a good time to draw up a will and select a guardian to care for the children should you and your spouse die.

As the glow of the first weeks after delivery passes and reality sets in, you'll be wondering how you could ever have imagined being able to afford a child. Already, your budget is stretched thin. Those were Christine's thoughts after she and her husband, Jim, brought home their daughter, Cheyenne. How did they survive on $29,000 a year? They got creative.

The parents-to-be put out the word to friends and relatives that they would welcome hand-me-down clothing and furniture for the baby, and people were happy to comply by unloading baby stuff they no longer needed or wanted. Christine and Jim picked up the few odds and ends they didn't have at thrift stores and yard sales. Christine bought clothing for Cheyenne that was a couple of sizes larger than necessary so the baby wouldn't grow out of the little duds right away.

Christine had always assumed she would use disposable diapers until she investigated the cost. Disposable diapers cost from $25 to $35 a week; hiring a diaper service that would deliver 80 to 100 nappies a week cost only $15. She quickly made the switch.

Jim was put in charge of combing the local newspaper for coupons on baby items, such as baby food and formula, which saved the couple several dollars a week. By the end of the year, they calculated that coupons had saved them a total of $123.

Following the law also saved the couple money. Jim went to the local Social Security office and signed up baby Cheyenne for a Social Security card. Doing that saved the couple $50—the law states that if you fail to register a child for a Social Security card within one year of the child's birth, parents will be fined $50.

Because state law mandates that children riding in cars be strapped into a child's car seat, Jim also visited the local police department, where he arranged to lease a child's car seat for about $5, saving the couple the $60 to $100 it would have cost to buy one.

But the expenses for Cheyenne were relatively small. Parents with older children, like Mike and Cara, can tell you that as a child grows, so does her needs and wants, and the bills associated with those. Andrew, six, and Aubrey, eight, constantly challenge their parents' efforts to save money. It seems they want everything their friends have or that they see advertised on Saturday morning TV.

Mike and Cara agreed to take a vow of restraint. That's the only way they can pay for daily living expenses and squeeze money from their weekly paychecks for savings. The parents set rules about how many new toys each child can have in a month and avoid the temptation to shower them with expensive gifts and clothing. Instead, they buy used toys at yard sales and shop at discount stores when they want new items. They save scraps of odds and ends from around the house—paint, wood, cardboard, empty soda bottles, and juice cans—and encourage Andrew and Aubrey to make their own fun creations.

Cara formed a babysitting cooperative with other mothers in the neighborhood, and they barter babysitting time, eliminating the cost of paying for a sitter. She also saves money by cutting Andrew's and Aubrey's hair herself and makes their Halloween costumes.

To teach their children financial responsibility, Cara and Mike give the kids a weekly allowance of $3 each. When the children lobby for an item their parents choose not to buy, the adults advise them to save their allowance and buy it themselves. Not only does it save the parents money, it has started the children on the lifelong habit of saving.

Saving for College

Seven months ago, Heather and Don had a baby. Little Diana Michelle is a joy, but she's an expensive proposition, too. The proud parents are having a tough time meeting living expenses on Don's $17,000-a-year salary as an auto mechanic and Heather's $12,000 annual income as a video store manager. The mortgage, food bills, and utilities must be paid, along with pediatrician expenses, hospital bills, and items for the baby. Lately, the baby's grandparents have started nagging the couple about saving for Diana's college education. That sounds about as reasonable to Heather and Don as asking them to scale Mount Kilimanjaro. In a weekend. Wearing sneakers.

Renee, a divorced mother with two sons, 11 and 14 years old, can't seem to get out of debt, despite her $36,000-a-year income. Now her older son, an A student, is talking about going to Harvard someday, and the younger boy also hopes to go to college. Renee doesn't want to deflate their hopes, but at the same time, her financial situation makes her wonder if it will be possible for her to provide a college education for her children.

Unless you have an income over $100,000 and plenty of secure assets, you are bound to be concerned about providing for your child's college education. Even wealthy families start to sweat it out if they have two or more children attending private schools at the same time.

College education is a big ticket item; in fact, next to a mortgage, it is one of the largest expenses a family will ever have. Gone are the days when a student could work his way through college selling magazine subscriptions door-to-door. In addition to tuition, there's a host of other things you have to pay for. Room and board, fees (student activity, laboratory, library), books, equipment and supplies, travel to and from school, entertainment, and living expenses can add thousands of dollars to the cost of sending your child through school. Today, the average cost of one year at a public college is about $9,000, and the price tag is double that for private institutions. And if your child plans to go to an elite school, as Renee's son does, one year can cost $26,000.

Those figures sound staggering enough to already overloaded parents, and they are expected to keep increasing. If inflation rises, college costs will skyrocket even more. By the year 2000, four years will cost $41,000 at a public college, $105,000 at a private college, and $148,000 at an Ivy League school. Those figures could double by 2012.

STRING SAVER #26

Join with neighbors to buy fuel oil. Buying in larger quantities can save from 5 to 25 cents per gallon.

As daunting as these numbers seem, though, parents should take heart. Their salaries also will be rising. And almost all families qualify for financial aid in the form of scholarships, loans, grants, or jobs on campus. In fact, three-fourths of all college students finance half of their college expenses through a financial aid package, which often consists of a variety of forms of assistance. The average student receives about $3,000. If your family income is $50,000 or less and you have few assets other than your home, your child will very likely receive some form of financial aid. If your income is above that, your child still could qualify if you have two or more children attending college at the same time. Depending on your circumstances, a financial aid package could cover 65 to 100 percent of the expenses (but a package that covers 100 percent of expenses is very rare).

But no family can determine well ahead of time whether their child is going to qualify for a financial aid package that foots the entire bill. That is rare. Instead, assume that the college will expect you to kick in your fair share. That means you have to get started on your savings strategy—now.

Get Your Act Together So You're Ready When They Are

Saving for the college education of one child, and possibly several, can seem so overwhelming that some parents just don't do it, hoping that "something will come up" to rescue them when the time arrives. But magical financial aid packages don't fall from the sky, nor do good fairies leave college funds tucked under Junior's pillow. College planning takes effort and commitment, put into effect as early in the child's life as possible. An old saying goes that the longest journey begins with one small step. So too with saving for college.

Heather and Don could start a college fund by asking all their relatives to give Diana Michelle money or savings bonds rather than gifts for birthdays and holidays. The cash could be placed in a special savings account until there is enough to meet a minimum requirement for a certificate of deposit or other low-risk investment. As more funds are generated, they could make more aggressive higher-yield investments by gradually adding stocks, bonds, and mutual funds. The parents also could take out a whole life insurance policy with a cash value feature, which will grow gradually over the years. When Diana Michelle is ready to pack her trunk for college, the policy could be cashed in.

STRING SAVER #27

Instead of buying new shoes, repair the ones you've got. Under $20 buys you new soles, heels, and a shine.

Renee could take a similar approach, but she could pad the college account by activating some of the cost-saving measures sprinkled around this book, and putting the difference, the actual dollars and cents, in a jar marked "cash for college," or planting the money in a savings account until it grows. She should set a realistic savings goal—perhaps $20 a week—so she won't get too frustrated or discouraged if she falls short. When she has enough, Renee could purchase zero-coupon Treasury bonds, which usually are deeply discounted. At some long-term maturity date, the bond will pay the face value.

If her ex-husband owes her overdue child support, now is the time to start collecting. It may even be appropriate for them to revise their settlement agreement so that he is held responsible for paying some of his sons' college expenses. If she continues to flounder, she should seek the help of a reputable financial planner.

The Best Ways to Save for College

There are six primary ways to save for your child's education and, at the same time, stay ahead of inflation and rising tuition costs.

1. *Stocks.* Investing in stocks is the best way to accumulate a reserve, because, for the past 70 years, they have consistently outperformed every other type of investment. Invest in stocks, however, only if your child is ten or more years away from going to college. The risk of losing money will then be reduced over the long haul.

2. *Mutual funds.* A diversified portfolio of mutual funds also offers good potential for growth. Again, diversity is the key to success. Because you don't want to be stuck with just one fund that turns out to be a clunker, invest in as many as five different types of funds, such as a balanced fund, a municipal bond fund, and an international stock fund. Although many funds require a $1,000 minimum to get started, you can, in some cases, negotiate with the fund company to waive that requirement in exchange for a savings plan that automatically deducts $25 or $50 a month from your salary.

3. *U.S. savings bonds.* The returns on savings bonds have hovered around 7 percent. Not spectacular, but not bad, either. And you have the added assurance of knowing the funds are

STRING SAVER #28

Shop around for a hospital if you need elective surgery or treatment. Hospitals are big business, and like any business, they charge differently for their services. Be an educated consumer. Ask about accreditation, which will guarantee at least a minimum of competence. Compare costs for rooms, tests, and surgery. Some states have agencies that can provide you with this information. In Pennsylvania, for example, both the People's Medical Society in Allentown and The Pennsylvania Health Cost Containment Council in Harrisburg keep tabs on the costs of physicians and hospitals.

Women Need to Plan

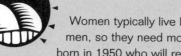

For women, financial planning is doubly important than it is for men. In almost every respect, women begin at a disadvantage compared to men.

Women typically live longer in retirement than men, so they need more savings. Of Americans born in 1950 who will reach age 65, women are expected to live to age 87, six years longer than men, on average. More than half the women over 65 are expected to spend time in a nursing home, a move that wipes out the savings of many retirees.

There are other reasons why women need to save more for retirement. They generally earn less than men—about 76 cents to the dollar, although the gap narrows with workers in their twenties. Women also have less disposable income to save for future needs. Because many women take time off from work to raise children, they tend to work fewer years than men, reducing future Social Security and pension benefits.

Fewer than a third of women employed in the private sector are covered by pensions. That's because they tend to work in low-wage, nonunion jobs in small firms in the service sector—jobs that are the least likely to provide retirement benefits.

Despite their financial handicaps, though, women are less prepared for retirement than men. Although they typically save for children's education, vacations, and major purchases, such as cars or houses, retirement is usually low on the priority list.

If you're a woman, start saving as early as you can. Make a special effort to educate yourself about ways to invest, and use the resources provided throughout this book to get yourself involved in personal finance. Feeling comfortable about money is a state-of-mind kind of thing, and an effective savings plan is as easy to follow as an exercise program. Save whenever and wherever you can, and give yourself the security and peace of mind a healthy financial picture can bring.

"safe." Another plus is that if you redeem the bonds to cover college tuition and your family meets income guidelines, the interest on the bonds is exempt from federal income taxes.

4. *Zero-coupon Treasury bonds.* These can be bought at deep discounts and are considered very safe investments. The future value and maturity dates are determined ahead of time so parents are aware of exactly how much money they will have for college. The downside: Parents must pay tax on interest every year even though they won't actually receive the interest, in the form of a lump sum, until the maturity date.

5. *Life insurance.* Although the rate of growth on cash value policies is lackluster, life insurance does provide another alternative for creating a college fund, especially if the family has difficulty saving money through another means. Parents can borrow from most life insurance policies or can cancel the policy when the funds are needed for college tuition.

6. *Home equity loans.* Many people borrow money through a home equity line of credit—also known as a second mortgage—to pay for college. The interest on home equity loans tends to be lower than on many other types of bank loans, and the interest you pay is tax-free.

If you are thinking about withdrawing money from your retirement accounts to pay for college—stop. If you do that, you will owe income taxes on the money withdrawn and you will have to pay a 10 percent tax penalty on the money if you are under the age of 59 1/2. In addition, those funds will have to appear on your child's financial aid form and could affect his ability to get a good assistance package. Finally, ask yourself if you're planning on working forever. Without a retirement fund, you'll be punching that time clock until you keel over.

STRING SAVER #29

Compare foods by unit price when you're shopping for groceries. If the label doesn't show it, divide the price of the product by its net weight of volume. Then, compare unit prices for the same product. What once seemed like a good deal may not look so great any more.

The Name Game

Once you have decided on the type of portfolio you want to build for a college education fund, the question is: Whose name should the fund be in, the parents' or the child's?

By law, minors cannot own securities (not even mutual fund shares), but the Uniform Gifts to Minors Act (UGMA) provides a way to invest on behalf of your child—and you can use the money to pay for college. You can open a UGMA account in your child's name (with you or another adult as custodian) with as little as $50, and contribute as much as you want to. One advantage to these accounts is that income up to $1,000 earned from them (dividends or capital gains) is taxed at a lower rate than the usual income tax rate. Be careful though, because income over that $1,000 is taxed at the parents' rate. When the child becomes 14 years of age, her income is then taxed at their own rate, which is usually 15 percent.

Financial planners typically caution parents against putting the money in the child's name, for a couple of reasons. First, when college financial aid officers look at a family's complete financial picture, they also consider any assets owned by the student, including funds from a portfolio. Students are expected to use up to 35 percent of their own funds to foot the bill for college, while parents are expected to contribute no more than 6 percent. Obviously, if Billy's name were on the fund, a huge chunk would be taken out to appease the financial aid gods. In addition, when the child reaches the age of 18, the funds are his, to do whatever he likes with. If backpacking in Tibet, moving to Las Vegas, or buying a fancy sports car sounds more enticing than going to college, Billy can do just that, because the money is his.

Kids Can Help Out

Given the high cost of tuition today, the entire burden for payment shouldn't fall on the parents. There are steps that students also can take to ease the blow:

- *Attend a community college.* Cash-conscious students who spend their first two years attending a community college can save almost 50 percent on their tuition bill and still receive a solid education in the basic courses, which is what they would be studying anyway in their freshman and sophomore years at a four-year college. In addition to tuition, community college students, most of whom are commuters, don't have to pay for a dormitory room, a meal plan, and other costs associated with on-campus living. In addition, commuting cuts down on the number of parties going on and allows students to concentrate more on studies, which should make parents happy. Community college students who do well academically also are more likely to get a favorable financial aid package, maybe even an academic scholarship to the four-year college, and that will help trim the bottom line. One drawback is that some community college courses may not be transferable to the four-year college, so the money paid for them would be wasted. Students should be very careful about checking whether credits are transferable to the university of their choice before taking classes at the community college.

- *Attend a public school.* Public universities may not have the cachet of an Ivy league school, but they don't have the high price tag, either. Generally, private colleges cost twice as much as public universities; they also are subject to larger one-shot tuition hikes. And educational experts confirm that the name of a high-quality public institution will look better on your resume than a grade B private school.

- *Live on campus and eat in the cafeteria.* It may not be cool, but going the dorm and cafe route will put your child financially ahead of peers who opt to live off-campus and buy their meals. Dormitories are the most economical housing option for college students, unless they are splitting the cost of off-campus housing with a horde of other people. Even then, living off-campus can be more expensive because students don't have to worry about paying for utilities, trash collection, and other related expenses when they live in the dorm. Meal plans also are a must for budget-minded college students, unless they are skipping meals and eating elsewhere. If they're not eating the

STRING SAVER #30

Dry clothing in consecutive loads, while heat is still retained inside the dryer.

meals that have been paid for as part of the plan, check to see whether the plan can be dropped or retabulated.

- *Work a part-time job.* When students are able to handle some of their own expenses, it takes a little weight off mom and dad. On- and off-campus jobs usually are plentiful while classes are in session. They may even provide some experience to add to a resume and contacts who can help when the student is ready to venture out into the real world.

- *Get good grades.* Students who earn below a C often are required to take the course over and, of course, that means paying for it again. Good study habits pay off in more ways than one.

- *Buy and sell used textbooks.* These days, a single textbook can easily cost $50, $80, or even more for select courses. Multiply that by the average number of five courses—some of them requiring more than one book—and you've got a hefty bill. But most campuses have a buy-back policy at the end of the semester. If the course is being offered again and the same text is being used, the campus bookstore will refund a portion of the original purchase price. Students who signed up for the course in the future can purchase the used texts and save money, too.

- *Carpool.* Students who are driving home for weekends or vacations can save money by carpooling and splitting expenses with their buddies.

- *Join ROTC.* Although your child may not relish the idea of wearing fatigues to class one day a week and practicing his salute, joining the Reserve Officers' Training Corps (ROTC) is one way to help pay for college. High school students or graduates who are college-bound can apply for this program. They can receive financial assistance that covers full tuition (up to $75,000), textbooks, and fees. They can also receive a subsistence allowance of $100 per month for up to 40 months.

- *Pay your way through.* Students who don't qualify for grants or scholarships and don't want to be saddled with loan debt when they graduate opt to take courses only as they can afford them. This is not the route for someone who is in a rush to finish because, depending on the student's financial picture, it could take more than four years to complete a college education. But the payoff is a debt-free graduation day and the satisfaction of knowing you're one step ahead on the road to long-term financial security.

Divorce

Almost half of all marriages end in divorce. Obviously, this takes a huge emotional toll on the couple, which lasts for years. But the financial toll exacted by divorce can last even longer, for decades or even the rest of their lives.

When couples are in the midst of splitting, attending to their emotional pain usually takes precedence over money. It is crucial, however, to carefully consider the financial ramifications of the divorce in order to lessen their impact. If you don't feel able to take an objective stance and look at the long-term financial picture, find an attorney or financial adviser to help you.

The first and best way for couples in trouble to save money is not to divorce at all. It really is true that two can live as cheaply as one. Middle- and lower-income couples who divorce often experience a dramatic decline in their standard of living as the income that used to support one household must be stretched to support two. Stay-at-home spouses may find themselves having to take a job, and if they haven't worked outside the home for awhile, they may have difficulty finding a position that pays well. The primary breadwinner—still the husband, more often than not—will find a huge chunk of his paycheck, sometimes 50 percent or more, being taken for alimony and, if applicable, child support.

DAY CARE DISCOUNT

Licensed day care facilities, often run by stay-at-home moms in their homes, typically charge 20 percent less than larger, licensed facilities. Of course, you need to carefully **inspect** any day care facility before sending your child there. Many day care programs give a discount to parents who bring more than one child.

Divorce is expensive. A typical divorce can costs thousands of dollars, sometimes more than a wedding. Why does it cost so much?

- *The lawyers.* Attorneys specializing in divorce often charge $200 an hour or more for their services. The more a couple wrangles and quibbles and takes up an attorney's time, the more their divorce is going to cost. One couple, legendary in a Pennsylvania divorce court, fought bitterly for months over who should get their set of monogrammed bath towels. (The wife eventually prevailed.) The fee they paid their attorneys to fight the battle could have bought dozens of sets of towels before it was all over. Lesson: Try to settle the matter as quickly and amicably as possible.

STRING SAVER #31

Don't buy large quantities of over-the-counter medication if you aren't going to use them in the near future. A bottle of 500 aspirin may sound like a good deal at first, but if you don't use the medication by the expiration date, it will go bad. Buy only what you think you will use.

To reduce legal fees even further, consider using a divorce mediator to help you thrash out some of the details before taking them to an attorney, thus saving time and money. Mediators, whose services are listed in the Yellow Pages, charge from $50 to $150 an hour, depending on their training and the region of the country.

Couples with no children and few assets who are parting on relatively good terms should think about a do-it-yourself divorce. In some states, paralegals will fill out the necessary documents for $200 or less and file them with the appropriate courts. They give no legal advice, as an attorney would, but they will help you get an economical divorce that is perfectly legal.

- *Alimony and child support.* Alimony is a court-ordered payment by one spouse (usually the one with the higher income) to the other for a defined period of time that can extend from one to several years. Child support is a court-ordered payment by one parent to the other, "custodial" parent, to cover child care expenses until the children are 18, in some states, or 21 in others. The amount of the payment varies with the payer's income, the number of children, their ages, whether the custodial parent is working, and a host of other factors. Generally, though, alimony and child support payments can equal between one-third to one-half of the payer's income.

There are few ways to cut costs here, since the law regulates how much will be paid. Whether you are the payer or the one being paid, have a reputable, knowledgeable attorney attempt to get you the best deal possible. Help your attorney accomplish this by going through your records and thoroughly documenting your living expenses, everything from the mortgage to magazine subscriptions. The more a judge knows about the details of your financial history, the more likely you will be to get a fair arrangement.

One note: Alimony payments are tax-deductible for the payer. The recipient, however, must include them as gross income. Child support is not tax deductible by the payer, but the recipient does not have to reveal it as income.

Therefore, if you are the payer, it is to your financial advantage to pay more in alimony and less in child support; if you are the recipient, you benefit if more money is paid in child support and less in alimony.

- *Hidden expenses.* There are countless expenses involved with setting up new households: rent or another mortgage, furniture, utility bills,

CONSIDER PREPAYMENT

A growing number of colleges are allowing parents to prepay their child's college tuition years before admission. If you are enrolling a newborn, the cost of prepayment might be $50 a month; for a preteen, $200 a month. The advantage is that the parent pays at today's rate and doesn't have to worry about inflation making their child's tuition out of reach. In addition, the money will be refunded if you select another school. The disadvantage, however, is that the refund is only the principal and does not include any interest that would have accrued over the years if the same sum had been invested.

and many others. If a spouse needs to find a job, there are expenses attached to the job hunt: new clothing, and perhaps a car. If both parents are already working, there may be new child care expenses. The list goes on forever.

If possible, you and your spouse should sit down together and closely examine where expenses can be trimmed or where sharing might still be possible. One couple, who were still on good terms years after their divorce, split the cost of newspaper and magazine subscriptions and swapped reading material when they were finished.

As you hash out the details of your divorce, reexamine your position regarding investments and insurance with respect to your new status and obligations. If you were paying for a life insurance policy that would reimburse your spouse in the event of your death, you probably will want to cancel that.

In addition:

- Change the names of beneficiaries on your will, life insurance policy, pension, and other important documents to reflect the change in your marital status.

- Take your name off of joint accounts and cancel credit cards and phone cards in joint names. If you don't, your spouse legally will be able to continue using them and leave you financially responsible for payment. .

NOW you're saving for RETIREMENT?

CHAPTER NINE

It may be a ways off, but as they say, "it's never too early to plan." Set aside a **nest egg** *for yourself to enjoy life after the working day is through.*

Chad is one of the lucky ones. He graduated at the top of his class from a good university and within months, the talented 23-year-old photographer landed a staff job at a metropolitan newspaper, beating out a long line of competitors. Of course, he doesn't plan to shoot accident scenes and political rallies forever, but right now, he's enjoying the ride.

Enjoying it a little too much, some might say. Slim, dark-haired, and never without female companionship, Chad likes to buy the snazziest clothes at the mall, take weekend trips sailing or skiing, and pick up presents for his girlfriends. He's bought a new car, and despite his free spending, has managed to put away enough each week for a down payment on a small home in a good part of town, thanks to an automatic payroll deduction plan at work.

It seems like Chad has everything, except a stable financial future. His immediate job prospects look bright. But like many younger people, Chad's concept of saving for the future stretches to about five years from now. He can't conceive of being 30 years old, much less 60. Retirement is a concept he associates with his perennially suntanned, bingo-playing grandparents in Florida. Tell Chad that some day he will retire too, and he thinks he's just as likely to sprout wings and fly. Approach the concept of saving for retirement with Chad and he zones out.

Start Early

Chad has fallen into a common trap: He believes retirement planning is for old people, the ones over 40. In fact, financial experts have raised a loud and consistent drumbeat about the absolute necessity for people to begin planning for retirement in their 20s or 30s. Preferably, retirement planning should begin when you get your first job. If you don't start when you're young, you probably won't be able to afford a retirement. Forget about your plans to globe-trot or buy a villa in Hawaii where you can whoop it up and be the oldest surfer on the planet.

You're much more likely to wind up like the manager of a construction business who, after he retired, realized he didn't have enough funds to meet even basic expenses and was forced to take a part-time job as a supermarket checkout clerk. Fast food restaurants and department stores are filled with elderly employees who ignored retirement planning when they were young. The only difference between an old man and an elderly gentleman is adequate income.

Retirement is expensive. To look at the retired set, you might think they've got it made. Their houses and other major debts usually are paid off by that time, their kids are grown, they don't need a lot of fancy clothes, and businesses are forever offering senior citizen discounts on products and services. But while some expenses decrease in retirement, others become greater, such as the amount of money spent on travel and medical bills. And, cross your fingers, you're not going to die right after you get your gold watch. The average person who retires at 65 can expect to live another 17 to 20 years without a paycheck.

If you don't want your lifestyle to decline dramatically when you retire, you have to plan on a strategy that will guarantee you receive 70 to 80 percent of your last annual paycheck. If you are earning $80,000 in the year before retirement, you will need about $64,000 a year to be able to live in a comparable style afterward. Multiply that by 20 years and you'll see that you need a whopping $1,280,000 saved to keep up the style to which you've become accustomed. Before you start to hyperventilate, realize that there are ways that the average person can amass that amount without resorting to bank robbery. One of them is starting to save as early as possible so that you can let compound interest do its happy work.

If you are 25 years old and earn $25,000 a year, you could put $2,500 a year into retirement savings with a return of 8 percent a year, and you will have $1,057,718 in 40 years. But if you wait until you're 35 to start saving, you'll have to put aside $10,115 to reach the same amount.

The concept of early retirement planning was not lost on Brooke, a 28-year-old department manager at a utility company. She began putting 5 percent of her $43,000 yearly salary into her company's tax-free 401(k) plan. Her employer matches each of her contributions with 50 cents. Today, she has $5,000 saved. Brooke plans to become more aggressive with her retirement savings and next year will contribute 8 percent of her salary. If she continues to do that, she will have approximately $1.7 million by the time she's 65. If Brooke chooses to continue working for awhile after the age of 65, she will be able to save even more.

Gotta Getta Goal!

It's not enough to have a hazy idea about how you would like your retirement to be. You must map out a specific plan and write it down so that you can refer to it from time to time and assess your progress.

First, decide what kind of lifestyle you want when you retire. Do you want to travel a great deal or are you planning on a more modest, settled way of life? Then, using that as a guide, decide how much income you will want or need during retirement, based on today's dollars. Set two goals: a bare-bones amount that you could get by on and another that would cover your ideal lifestyle.

Next, figure out how much you need to save to fund your retirement. Obviously, if you plan to retire early you'll need more than if you work until you are 65 or older.

The farther you are from retiring, the more difficult precise calculations will be. If you haven't already done so, talk with your employer about what you can expect from the employer-sponsored retirement plan. Most companies that offer plans send out yearly statements to employees telling them where their retirement funds stand.

Call the Social Security Administration at (800) 772-1213 and ask for a Personal Earnings and Benefits Statement. It's a simple form that you fill out and return. Within a few weeks, you will receive a statement of your complete earnings history along with estimates of your benefits for retirement at age 62, at 65, and at 70.

When you have estimated your earnings from your pension and Social Security, calculate how much you need to invest in order to meet your financial goal for retirement. Don't forget to figure in the effects of taxes and inflation; it's imperative to consider how these twin devils will run rampant over your hard-earned money. If you are in the 28-percent tax bracket, for instance, subtract 28 percent from the total you had in mind and see what's left. Then, take that figure, and consider how an average inflation rate of 4 percent will cut its spending power. If you think you will need $100,000 in today's dollars to fund your retirement, you'll actually need $219,000 two decades from now.

Social Security?

The first thing many people think about when they consider their retirement income is Social Security. On Fridays when they receive The Check, senior citizens flock to banks and stores and restaurants to enjoy the fruits of their labor. Since the 1930s, the federal government has helped us save for retirement by deducting an ever-increasing sum from our paychecks—today it is 7.6 percent—to be put into the till designated Social Security. The money currently deducted is used to fund checks senior citizens receive today. The system also pays funds to people who are widowed or disabled. In turn, the government promises that when we retire, we will get back the money we paid in.

For younger people, there are problems with this. Social Security checks, which are based on a portion of your overall earnings, are not enough to live on in retirement. People who retired in 1995 collected an average of $14,000 a year in Social Security. In addition, people who were born in 1960 or later will not be able to collect full benefits until they are 67 years old; if they retire earlier, they will receive only 70 percent of their total benefits.

Taking Control: Pension Plans

Since younger workers cannot count on the Social Security system to fund their total retirement, they must take control of their own future and plan for it to an extent that no previous generation ever has. The best way to do this is through a tax-deferred pension plan that allows you, or you and your employer, to contribute funds that are free from taxation until they are withdrawn.

- *401(k)*. There is a lot of buzz lately about a hot little pension plan called the 401(k), and a growing number of employers offer them. Money invested in 401(k) accounts in this country has grown from $55 billion to $750 billion over the last ten years. If your company has a 401(k) plan, run, don't walk, to your benefits office to sign up.

It works like this: Your employer sets up the 401(k) plan and deposits a percentage of your salary in it (usually 2 to 10 percent). This money can be invested in a number of investment options including stocks, bonds, and mutual funds. The employer often matches the employee's contribution and pads the retirement coffers even more.

The law allows you and the company together to contribute up to 25 percent of your after-tax salary, but no more than $9,300 per year. You can begin withdrawing from the fund without paying a 10-percent penalty when you are 59 1/2 years old.

The down side of 401(k)s is that, because the money is invested, what you receive during retirement can fluctuate. There also is the risk of loss, although the law allows employees to shift their investments once every quarter. The mutual funds you invest in charge operating expenses of about 2 percent, which is taken from your capital.

Still, there are several reasons why people think 401(k)s are so nifty. Because the money is deducted from your salary automatically, saving is a breeze, and you are left with less income to pay taxes on right now. You don't have to pay taxes on any of the money in the fund until you withdraw it at retirement. And, if you leave the company, you can take the money with you and deposit it into another tax-deferred account.

The importance of depositing money in a tax-deferred account like the 401(k) cannot be stressed enough. If you are making $60,000 at the age of 35 and you put away 6

INVEST NOW

This chart assumes that you will invest $2,000 a year and earn 5 percent on your money after taxes.

Years Until Retirement	You Will Have
40	$253,680
30	139,522
20	69,439
10	26,414

percent of your salary in an account that is taxed but pays 8 percent interest, by age 65 you will have $283,925. But if the same amount is put into a 401(k) and your employer kicks in another 3 percent, you will have $857,608.

401(k)s also give workers the option to increase the amount they save. If you put aside $100 a month for 20 years at 8 percent interest, you will have $57,111. If you add $100 a month every year after for the next 18 years, you will have $370,928.

If absolutely necessary, your 401(k) can serve as a buffer in times of financial hardship. You can take out a loan of up to half the account balance, not to exceed $50,000. The loans are charged interest and must be paid back within a designated time, usually not more than five years. If it is not repaid on time, the outstanding balance is taxable and subject to a 10 percent early withdrawal penalty.

• *Individual Retirement Accounts (IRAs).* In 1981, the federal government noticed that the amount of money most Americans were saving for their retirement was alarmingly small. IRAs, another type of tax-deferred retirement plan, were created to give people incentive to save. Today, IRAs, along with 401(k)s, are among the most popular retirement savings plans around.

The law allows individuals to invest up to $2,000 a year in an IRA account; if you have a spouse who doesn't work, you can invest up to $2,250. If you don't have a company pension plan, you can deduct the full amount you contributed to the IRA. If you do participate, you can still deduct a portion of it, depending on your income. You can set up IRAs through banks, stockbrokers, credit unions and mutual fund companies.

As with 401(k)s, you cannot withdraw the funds before you are 59 1/2 without a 10-

percent penalty, although the law requires that you withdraw all the money by the age of 70 1/2. If you need money from your IRA to pay a bill, such as college tuition, before you are 59 1/2 and want to avoid the penalty, you can set up a plan to withdraw money on a fixed schedule for no more than five years.

If you want to transfer funds from one IRA plan to another, or add funds from a different retirement plan to an IRA, that is called a rollover. If you roll over funds within 60 days, you will not be taxed. However, if you have the funds in your possession for more than 60 days without depositing it in the IRA, the funds will be considered income and will be taxed.

- *Simplified Employee Pensions (SEPs)*. SEPs are retirement plans sponsored by employers in which the employer contributes up to $30,000 or 5 percent of compensation, whichever is less. Also, any employee may contribute an extra $2,000 each year.

- *Keoghs*. If you are self-employed, you can set up a retirement plan called a Keogh through banks, stockbrokers, and mutual fund companies and contribute a percentage of your income tax-deferred as long as it remains in the account. Keogh money can be invested in a variety of accounts, including stocks, bonds, mutual funds, and money markets.

When 32-year-old Stephanie decided to quit her job as a paralegal at a law firm, she had accumulated $11,000 in her 401(k) plan. She planned to start her own paralegal business and was tempted to use the pension money as start-up capital; after all, retirement seemed a very long time away and she had immediate financial needs. But a financial adviser convinced her that if she used the money, it would be taxed substantially and not only would she have no retirement funds, but she still would have less start-up capital than she needed. Instead she rolled over the money into an IRA account and was able to borrow money from relatives at a very low rate of interest to launch the business.

- *Defined Benefit Plan*. This is the kind of pension plan our parents had, if their company offered one. With a defined benefit plan, the company makes all of the contributions to the employee's retirement plan, and you sit back and relax until you collect at retirement. The advantages, of course, are that poor savers don't have to lift a finger to stockpile the money, and employees will know exactly how much money they will be getting on retirement day.

But this paternalistic system, which is rapidly disappearing, puts all of its eggs in one basket. If the company has financial problems, your pension could be in jeopardy. In addition, employees have no say in how much is contributed or how it is invested. If you have a defined benefit plan, cheer. But also take control of your own destiny by setting up an IRA and an investment portfolio.

Investments and Annuities

In addition to pension plans, investments in stocks are an essential part of retirement planning, especially when you are younger. Stocks are the only investment with enough gusto to outpace inflation.

Financial experts say that people in their 20s and 30s should have 80 percent of their retirement portfolio invested in stocks. Because they have three or four decades before they leave the workforce, there is plenty of time to ride out the ups and downs of the market and still come out ahead. Past performance records show that a portfolio with 80 percent in stocks and 20 percent in bonds is likely to grow an average of 9 percent annually, with a possible return as high as 25 percent.

People who are heading into their 40s might want to tone it down just a bit, especially if they want to buy a home and fund a child's college education. With two to three decades to go before retirement, invest 70 percent of your portfolio in stocks, put 20 percent in corporate bond funds, and the rest in an international bond fund. The average rate of return should be about 8.75 percent.

As you reach 50 and beyond, your investments portfolio gradually will shift away from stocks to "safer" vehicles. Tax-deferred annuities—sold by insurance companies, financial planners, stockbrokers, and some banks—are another way to save for retirement. You begin by making a lump sum payment of $2,000 to $10,000, which the company invests in certificates of deposit, money market funds, and other vehicles. Some of the annuities have fixed rates of interest, while others have a variable rate.

While fixed rate annuities are secure, they get eaten up by inflation. Variable rate annuities may outpace inflation but are more volatile and there is more risk.

Until you retire, you can continue to deposit as much money as you like because there is no IRA-type cap. Taxes are deferred until you retire, but you cannot take a tax deduction for contributions, as you can with an IRA. And, while the IRA requires you to withdraw all funds by the age of 70 1/2, the annuity allows you to continue making deposits for as long as you want.

Remember, because the annuity is being managed by someone else, you will be charged administrative fees that could be as much as 3 percent of your contribution. The annuity is also only as solid as the company that is selling it. Check with Standard & Poor's before investing. Focus on companies with a rating of A or better.

Don't Hang It Up Too Soon

Some people say youth is wasted on the young. The young counter that retirement is wasted on the old. Who wants to work until they are so old that they don't have the energy, interest, or good health to enjoy all the free time that retirement offers? That way of thinking has led many Americans to take the vow of early retirement, meaning before age 65 and, in some cases, before 60. The problem is that many people don't start thinking about early retirement until they have hit their 50s. But they've been so busy meeting daily living expenses that they had little time to invest for retirement.

Tell a financial planner you want to retire early and stand back. Be prepared to suffer a blast of reasons why you should stay at your desk as long as possible. Unless you plan to die shortly after retirement, you might want to reconsider. Social Security benefits are reduced when you retire before 65. Pension plans, annuities, and IRAs may incur a penalty for early withdrawal. In addition, by cutting short your contributions and withdrawing money earlier, you have fewer funds to rely on in the future.

Although your tax burden will drop somewhat when you retire, your postretirement income will continue to feel the pinch from taxes. In addition, when employees leave their jobs before 65, they have to pay for their own health insurance until they reach

65 and become eligible for Medicare. Health insurance premiums paid by individuals can be several hundred dollars a month, as much or more than a car payment.

Many early retirees count on getting a part-time job to supplement their income. But, depending on the region of the country and the mix of businesses in your town, part-time jobs might not be plentiful. And few pay well or offer decent benefits.

Those who are not discouraged will want to keep two words in mind before they board the ship bound for early retirement: plan and sacrifice. People who are successful in early retirement began planning their break from the workaday world long before everyone else, and they stayed focused on building substantial savings.

Early retirement wannabes gear their lives toward their goals by sacrificing immediate gratification for long-term rewards. They adjust their lifestyles so they can live well beneath their means for as many years as possible: choosing to live in less expensive parts of the country, buying smaller homes and modest cars, skipping expensive vacations, and passing on material froufrous. Some even decide not to have children so they can have more money for retirement.

And the sacrificing doesn't stop once they are retired. Early retirees who survive comfortably continue to sacrifice and save after retirement to make their resources stretch as far as possible. Early retirement requires you to assess realistically your resources, both financial and emotional.

There's a case to be made for the psychological and emotional benefits of staying in the loop, too. Remaining active and involved as long as you can may pay you benefits even more valuable than the money you receive. So before you decide on an early retirement, weigh the pros and cons carefully. In the end, only you can make that final decision.

MAKE *the* mental *saving* SHIFT

CHAPTER TEN

We've all heard stories about this or that fast-track couple who have left behind their six-figure income, transformed their lifestyle, and are now living in a cabin doing something idyllic like growing apples for a living, getting by on an annual income that once would have equalled the price of their car. And they've never been happier.

The media latches on to these stories because they tap into our deepest fantasies and depict the escape from reality we dream about. But many of us were baptized on the altar of American consumerism, which drives our economy and our lives. The need to buy things is bred into us as deeply as the need to eat hamburgers and fries. If you work hard and feel the need to reward yourself now and then, you can still be faithful to your savings plan, as long as you make careful choices about how you spend your money.

The Best Approach to Financial Planning Starts with a Little Attitude Adjustment

• *Learn to be happy with what you've got.* Try to redefine your definition of success. Look around you; take stock of your possessions. Really see—maybe for the first time in a long time—all that you've got. It's probably more than you realized. Then ask yourself the ways in which you could enrich the quality of your life. Maybe the answer is to strengthen your relationship with people you care about or to find work that is spiritually rewarding. Those things have nothing to do with spending money, but they could be defined as true success. Take the focus off the way material things can make you happy, and find a sense of contentment in what you already have.

• *Live beneath your means.* If you spend less than you earn, you'll have extra cash to save and invest. You don't have to go overboard and become a Scrooge about every single penny. But saving when and where you can will bring you a sense of satisfaction when you realize it's helping you run your life instead of letting your life run you.

• *Simplify.* The less complexity you have to deal with, the fewer expenses you will have and the more money you'll have left over to invest. Rather than buying and maintaining a vacation home, take small frequent vacations. Go camping, visit national parks or historic sites. Pets are costly, so rather than having six dogs and three cats, love only one or two of each. Take little bites of the good life and you'll be able to taste more of it.

• *Determine your real needs versus your wants.* Before spending your hard-earned money, first satisfy your needs for food, shelter, and clothing. When they are taken care of, then turn to your wants and listen critically. Make careful choices about how you spend your money. Become a critical, aware shopper and make careful choices about how you spend your money.

- *Shift your thinking from earning-to-spend to spending-to-earn.* Many of us go to work every day thinking about how we'll spend our paychecks: the bills we'll pay, the possessions we'll buy, the trips we'll take. Doing that, we trap ourselves. We have to work in order to spend, then work some more to pay off what we've bought, and in the end, we have little to show for all our efforts. So little of what we buy increases in value or returns its worth to us. Before making a purchase, ask yourself what kind of a return you will get on your investment. Will the item increase in value? Will it truly enhance the quality of your life? Will it fulfill a real need, rather than a desire? If not, you may want to reconsider. Instead, take the money you would have used for the purchase and invest it. That can bring a real return.

- *If you have a problem, don't be too proud to ask for help.* Compulsive gamblers or shopaholics are extreme cases of people who need professional help to get their spending habits in line. But many others just need a helping hand to get them into the habit of budgeting and spending more wisely. Some communities have budget counselors, whose numbers can be found in the local telephone book. Don't be afraid to reach out. And when money gets tight, don't head for the hills when creditors call. Instead, communicate the situation to them and arrange to pay what you owe on an installment plan. Ignoring financial problems won't make them go away. Like interest, they compound and ultimately will jeopardize your future.

Live the Good Life on a Shoestring Budget

There are surprising ways to live a white-collar lifestyle on a blue-collar income. You can take luxury vacations, eat in expensive restaurants, and even live in high-priced neighborhoods with a little research and ingenuity. Here are some strategies for getting what you want out of life—even if you think you can't afford it:

- When you're looking for a home, don't automatically rule out your absolute first-choice neighborhood or community because you think it's above your means. Condo living has lots of advantages and is sometimes a real estate bargain. Living in a condo development gives you the advantages of an instant neighborhood, access to recreational facilities, and outdoor landscaping and maintenance services. It could be a ticket into that town with the great schools that otherwise would be out of your reach.

- Vacations can renew the spirit, help you put things in perspective, and give you a fresh outlook. But it's hard to enjoy them when they either cost more than you're comfortable with or make you compromise your standards to fit a tight budget. Pick the getaway of your dreams and just scale it down a bit. Instead of a week at an exclusive resort, go for three or four days. Midweek prices can be as much as one-third of the price of weekend rates. Some ski resorts sell half-day lift tickets at reduced prices—sleep late and ski in the afternoon for a truly relaxing few days. Take advantage of frequent-flier miles whenever you can.

- If you enjoy eating out but get nauseous when the check comes, treat yourself to a good restaurant every once in awhile anyway. By skipping the appetizer and dessert, you can cut the cost of the meal in half. If you can forego the alcohol, you can bring the tab down even further. Go for lunch: You get the same service, the same atmosphere, the same food, for a lot less money.

- Do you like the way you look in designer clothes? Don't settle for second-rate outfits that will only be worn by a hanger in the back of your closet. Go for the good stuff. Just do it on sale and with restraint. This actually may be an area where it pays to buy impulsively. If you see a sweater or dress that screams, "Buy me!" it's probably because it's the kind of thing you can see yourself wearing a lot. Try it on. If it looks great and makes you feel good, get it. One great expensive pair of jeans you wear over and over again is worth three pairs of bargain dumpy corduroy pants that don't do anything for you but cover your legs. Limit yourself to a budget, shop in the designer outlets, and stick to pieces that go with each other. Black goes with everything and doesn't need dry cleaning as much.

- Some people need a car that describes who they are or where they want to be. If that's important to you, there are ways to save money on this big purchase. Instead of buying a brand-new car, consider leasing one that's a year old. Corporations that lease cars for their executives exchange these cars every year for the latest models. The leasing companies will often re-lease these cars. They're in great condition and close to new. You get the car you want, but it costs a lot less than the new car. If this is still over your budget, think about buying a model that's several years old. The message you send to the world is, "I am a person of taste. I know what car to wear. I just can't afford it right now." And if you keep using the techniques out-lined throughout this book for investing and saving your money, it won't be long before you will be able to afford that car.

What Is Your Financial Personality?

Spender

You have a "can't-take-it-with-you" attitude that allows you to give yourself permis-sion to buy on impulse and spend too much. You buy whatever you want without thinking of the long-term consequences, spend too much on gifts, and eat out often at expensive restaurants. You're one step ahead of your creditors and have little saved.

Solution:

Create a planned spending program and eliminate impulse purchases. Figure out a monthly budget, leaving some leeway for buying fun things. Giving yourself a little "mad money" to fritter away will help you cut down on spending overall, rather than trying to go cold turkey, then binging when you feel the need to spend. Take some time before making decisions on major purchases, and consider all the angles before jumping in head first.

Worrier

You fret over every decision, whether it's about saving money or spending it. You find it difficult to make up your mind, and you stew over what other people might think. Indecision leads you to make poor purchases. For example, you buy an inexpensive gift for your mother, then change your mind and buy something more expensive. Ultimately, you've spent more money than you intended because you've now bought two gifts rather than one.

STRING SAVER #32

Ask your doctor if it is possible to have routine tests done before you're admitted to a hospital; this cuts down on the expense and may decrease the length of your stay.

Solution:

Work out an umbrella plan for spending, so that you don't have to agonize over each little decision. When you have a focus and a direction for your spending, all that you need to do when you have to make a decision is ask yourself whether it falls in line with your goals.

Saver

You know exactly how much money is in your wallet. You pay cash for a new car, shop the bargain stores, and stick to an organized budget. Savers, however, can cross the line into miserliness. You know this has happened when you start to deny yourself creature comforts just to accumulate money, and nothing gives you more pleasure than watching the numbers grow in your savings passbook.

Solution:

Lighten up a bit. Budgeting and saving are important, but so is enjoying life. Set aside some cash each month just for pleasure purchases—and use it.

SAVE *by* surfing *through* CYBERSPACE

CHAPTER ELEVEN
There is a wealth of information on the Internet for people who are dedicated to financial planning and saving money. **Forums,** *home pages, and chat areas can be guides for people who are creating financial road maps for their* **future years.**

It would be impossible to list every site related to personal finances. Instead,we have chosen several that are especially useful for novices. But before you log on, sign up with an Internet provider that offers a flat monthly fee for unlimited usage; hourly rates will undo your carefully planned budget.

Bonds

- Bonds Online. This site from Twenty-First Century Mutuals has Frequently Asked Questions (FAQ) sheets, ratings, advice on choosing a

bond broker, and news reports from Knight-Ridder.
http://www.bonds-online.com/

- Information from the Consumer Information Center. Provides information on buying Treasury securities and bonds.
http://gopher.gsa.gov/oo/staff/pa/cic/money/t-bills.txt

- Investment FAQ. This file covers 60 areas dealing with commonly asked questions about investments, especially stock market information.
http://www.cs.umd.edu/users/cml/invest-faq

- Savings Bond Calculator. Lets you calculate the exact value of your Series EE Savings Bond. Enter the year and month it was issued, the face value, and the redemption month. http://www.mmrsoft.com

Brokers

- eBroker. You can do your stock trading online. Fill out an application for the service and check out rate schedules. http://www.ebroker.com/

- National Discount Brokers. They can trade securities for a relatively low, flat-fee commission. They also have an online trading FAQ list, and more. http://www.pawws.secapl.com/ndb/

- Prudential Securities. Trades securities products, and offers market analyses and educational materials about investing. http://www.prusec.com/

- Quick & Reilly. Provides information about this discount brokerage and investment software. http://www.quick-reilly.com/

- Schwab Online. Describes services, and offers investment tips and a database of over 1,100 mutual funds. http://www.schwab.com/

Buying a House

- Homes and Land National Real Estate Database. Look for the best deals among 100,000 listings in 43 states. Search by type of property, state, or region. http://www.homes.com:8087/

- Homebuyers Fair. A diverse array of material for potential buyers, including mortgage quotes, consumer tips, and an apartment search feature.
http://www.homefair.com/home/

- Home buying tips. A worksheet for potential home owners that helps you ask all the right questions during your hunt and gives you the space you need to record information on properties you have visited.
http://www.hypervigilance.com/househunt.html

- Mortgage calculator. This form generates a list of first-year monthly payments and lifetime payments, broken down by interest and principal.
http://alfredo.wustl.edu/mort.html

- Mortgage rates by state. Gives you a way to compare and select the best mortgage deals around the country. Choose a region, then enter the amount of the mortgage and its length. A table pops up displaying current rates of mortgage brokers along with links to their Web pages.
http://www.microsurf.com/

- U.S. Consumer Information Center. Offers a collection of 11 pamphlets discussing how to buy and finance a home. Subjects include how to buy a home with a low down payment, adjustable rate mortgages, and mortgage vocabulary. Most of the pamphlets are free or cost 50 cents.
http://www.gsa.gov/staff/pa/cic/housing.htm

Consumer Tips

- Federal Trade Commission consumer brochures. This site provides brochures on a variety of consumer scams involving credit card marketing, wireless cable TV, infomercials, land sales, gemstones, and more.
http://www.webcom.com/~lewrose/brochures.html

- Shop! Information Services. A public service of the Women's Consumer Foundation, this site exposes companies that have been ripping off female consumers. Investigative reports are intended to save consumers money.
http://www.sis.org/

- Consumer Information Center. This U.S. government organization provides information on credit cards, investment fraud, and financial planning. http://www.pueblo.gsa.gov/

Credit Card Information

- Card Trak. Resource for finding credit cards with low rates, no annual fees, and other desirable features. Also provides a survey of credit cards and includes feature articles. http://www.cardtrak.com

- Credit card pamphlets from the U.S. Consumer Information Center. Pamphlets available include "Choosing and Using Credit Cards," "Solving Credit Problems," "The Card You Pick Can Save You Money," "Managing Your Debts," and others. http://webcrawler.com/select/bank.06.html

Financial Advice and Debt Counseling

- Alliance & Leicester. Provides tools for personal finances, including an online mortgage calculator. http://www.alliance-leicester.co.uk

- American Consumer Credit Counseling. A nonprofit organization for people with money problems trying to regain control of their personal finances. http://www.consumercredit.com/

- Bonehead Finance. No get-rich-quick schemes here, just down-to-earth advice on making the best of your financial situation. http://www.ourworld.compuserve.com/homepages/Bonehead_Finance/

- Consumer Credit Repair. Deals with credit repair, debt consolidation, personal finance, loans, and mortgages. http://www.repaircredit.com/

- Debt Counselors of America. Approved by the Internal Revenue Service, this site helps with debt and financial difficulties. http://www.dca.org/home.htm

- Deloitte & Touche Online. A guide to personal finance, taxes, and business. http://www.dttus.com/

- Household Budget Management. Offers basic information on family money management. http://www.excite.com/aol/Reviews/ Money_and_Investing/Personal_finance/Financial

- Money Guide. A gopher menu of how-to articles on personal finance, saving, investment strategies, credit cards, insurance, retirement planning, and other money-related topics. gopher://gopher.gsa.gov/11/cic/money

- *Moneywise*. Covers topics of personal finance news and saving strategies. http://www.moneywise.co.uk/

- Motley Fool Online Financial Forum. Designed to help users obtain a wide spectrum of financial information and discuss investing techniques. A very popular site; lively and easy to understand. http://www.fool. web.aol.com/fool_mn.htm

- Quicken Financial Network. Offers financial news and referral services, information about investments, insurance and banking, as well as sources for software. http://www.excite.com/index.html

Investments

- American Association of Individual Investors. An independent nonprofit group designed to assist individuals in becoming effective managers of their own money. http://www.AAIIMembr.com

- *Growth Stock Gazette*. The publication's mission is to find high-growth, high-return-on-equity stocks by seeking out companies with superior track records. http://home.navisoft.com/gsg/index.htm

- Standard & Poor's Investor Services. Register with this online service to access research and recommendations on individual companies, information on services and terms, and to read the S & P indexes. http://webcrawler.com/select/invest.97.html

- The Pristine Day Trader. A collection of daily investment advisory services. http://www.pristine.com/

- Woodbridge & Associates. Offers information on the profitability of your investments through emerging growth companies. http://www.calypso.com/woodbridge/

Insurance

- Insurance Information Institute's Internet site. Provides information on insurance and how it works. http://www.iii.org/

- Insurance News Network. Has FAQ files on questions relating to life, home, and auto insurance, as well as Standard & Poor's ratings. http://www.insure.com/

Mutual Funds

- Mutual Fund FAQ. A file of answers to common questions about mutual funds. http://www.moneypages.com/syndicate/faq/index.html

- Mutual Fund Investor's Center. This educational resource takes you from the basics of mutual fund investing to more sophisticated concepts. Also provides a list of fund companies. http://www.mfea.com/

Retirement Planning

- Retirement Zone. Tables and worksheets provided by Kiplinger Financial Services to help you calculate future earnings and expenses. http://www.bookpage.com/kiplinger/

- Social Security Online. This government site provides benefit information, statistics, and a directory of local Social Security offices. http://www.ssa.gov/

- Workplace Fidelity. Operated by Fidelity Online Investment Center, this is the largest Web site devoted to people who invest in workplace retirement plans. Includes 401(k) information and special sections for employees who work in the public, private, and nonprofit sectors. http://www.fidelityatwork.com/

Saving Money

- Consumer World: Bargains and Offers. Deals on cruises, accommodations, electronics, cameras, computers, and other consumer products. http://www.consumerworld.org/bargains.htm

- Frugal Corner. Newsgroups, consumer advice, coupons, recipes, tips on creative cooking on a budget, craft-making, and microbrewing. http://www.best.com/%7Epiner/frugal.html

- *Frugal Gazette.* Monthly newsletter that offers instruction on how to take control of your money. Discusses how even on a small budget you can afford to pay for a house, college education, vacations, new cars—and pay down debt. http://www.frugalgazette.com/

- Frugal Living Book List. A compendium of books for and about tightwads. http://pages.prodigy.com/ASCD29A/books.htm

- Frugal Tip of the Week. Fans of Amy Dacyczyn's now defunct *Tightwad Gazette* books and newsletters carry on the tradition by exchanging tips on living beneath their means. http://www.sooner.brightok.net/%7Eneilmayo/

- Julie's Frugal Tips. More hints for saving money. This site offers a Tip of the Week. http://www.sooner.brightok.net/~neilmayo/

- Miser's Gazette Homepage. Dedicated to saving money, time, resources, and effort employing miserly methods, penny-pinching plans, and frugal facts. http://www.ctsnet.com/miser/

- The Dollar Stretcher. Gary Foreman writes a weekly column for newspapers, but his work also is available by e-mail on request. http://www.stretcher.com/dollar/

- *The EConomic HOmemaker* (ECHO). A monthly newsletter dedicated to helping homemakers through money- and time-saving ideas, hints, personal stories, and budget-minded recipes. http://members.aol.com/theechohl/index.html/

- Toll-Free Stuff from Freebies Mall. Get a free booklet full of fun, low-cost activities for kids. http://www.pages.prodigy.com/ULDE89A/

Taxes

- CyberTax. A directory of links to state and federal tax laws and information. http://www.knight-hub.com/baez/

- The Tax Prophet. Robert L. Sommers, a San Francisco tax attorney, writes about tax planning techniques and provides interactive tax applications. http://www.taxprophpet.com/

GLOSSARY

accrued interest: Interest that has accumulated between the last interest payment and the purchase date of a bond.

aggressive growth fund: A mutual fund that invests in companies that are newer and more on the cutting edge than growth companies. These are relatively high-risk funds with potential for tremendous price increases and high rates of failure.

aggressive growth stock: Stock in a company that is small, but rapidly expanding, giving the investor the opportunity to attain above-average returns.

amortization: The systematic reduction of a financial obligation, such as a mortgage.

annual report: A document presented to stockholders once a year that includes information about how the company is doing. It contains the balance sheet, income statement, and statement of cash flows as well as discussions about the business.

annuity: An investment that guarantees a fixed income for the remainder of a person's lifetime in return for the payment of a premium.

anticipated income: Money you know you will receive in the future.

appreciate: To increase in value.

asset allocation: Investing in a mix of stocks, bonds, cash, and so on to achieve various goals.

balanced investments: Blending one or more of the investment categories. For example, you may put money in stocks, bonds, and a money market fund. The different investments carry different levels of risk.

bankruptcy: The condition in which corporations or individuals legally declare that they can not meet their financial obligations.

bear market: A declining stock market.

beneficiary: The person named in a policy to receive money or property after the death of the policyholder.

blue-chip stock: A high quality stock of a major company that generally has a long, unbroken record of earnings and dividend payments.

bond: A debt instrument issued by a company or governmental body to finance a certain aspect of its operation. When you buy bonds, you are lending money to the institution issuing the bond, and you are entitled to receive interest on that loan.

bond fund: A mutual fund that invests in bonds.

Bridal Registry Account: A Federal Housing Administration program that enables gift-givers to deposit money into an account to be used for the purchase of a home.

budget: A systematic plan for spending and saving your income over a definite period of time, based on your income and expenses.

bull market: A rising stock market.

capital gains tax: A tax levied on the profit you make from the sale of property.

cash equivalents: Short-term, highly liquid securities that can be turned into cash quickly, such as short-term certificates of deposit, money market funds, and Treasury bills.

cash value: The money a policyholder will get back if he gives up an insurance policy.

Certificate of Deposit: An arrangement whereby a depositor receives a fixed rate of return on the principal for a year or less. Because there is a penalty for early withdrawal of the principal, the interest rate is usually more than a savings account. CDs are issued by banks, credit unions, and savings and loan associations, and are generally insured by the FDIC (Federal Deposit Insurance Corporation) or the Federal Savings & Loan Insurance Corporation up to $100,000.

Certified Financial Planner (CFP): A financial adviser who has taken courses, passed exams, and has been certified by the Institute of Certified Financial Planners.

Certified Public Accountant (CPA): An accountant who has passed a series of exams and has met state requirements.

collateral: The assets put up by a borrower as a pledge for his loan. The collateral can be taken by the lender if the loan is not repaid.

collectible: An asset of limited supply that is bought in the hopes that it will increase in value.

common stock: A type of stock that entitles the owner to have voting rights in the corporation and a claim to what remains after all the creditors and preferred stockholders have been paid, if the company goes out of business.

compound interest: When a bank pays interest on both the principal and the interest in a savings account.

consolidated loan: A loan made to replace two or more outstanding loans.

contingencies: Unexpected expenses that cannot be budgeted but must be met, such as replacing a broken pair of glasses.

convertible term insurance: Term insurance giving the insured the right to exchange the policy for permanent insurance without showing evidence of his or her insurability.

corporate bond: Debt instruments issued by corporations as a means of raising money.

credit: Your power to borrow money based on your reputation for repayment, your net income, and your assets.

creditor: An individual or institution to whom money is owed.

current premium: What an insurance company is now charging or expects to charge for coverage.

decreasing term insurance: Insurance that provides for decreasing death benefits during the term of the insurance.

deep-discount broker: A broker who offers almost no services or advice, but who facilitates trades for a greatly reduced commission.

default risk: The risk that a company or other bond issuer will fail to pay on its debts.

deductible: 1. Describing an expense that can be used to reduce the amount of income tax liability. 2. The amount of money an insurance policyholder must pay before the insurance company provides benefits.

depreciation: Loss of value.

disability insurance: Insurance that pays the policyholder if he becomes unable to work due to an illness or injury.

discount broker: A broker who facilitates trades for a reduced commission without offering services and information.

discretionary income: The money you can spend as you please after you have paid bills and living expenses.

diversification: An investment strategy that relies on distributing investments among a variety of securities to minimize risk.

dividend: A payment issued by a company that distributes part of its profits and earnings to shareholders.

equity: 1. The value to you of a property after all mortgage, claims, and liens are paid off. 2. Common and preferred stock.

face value: The sum stated on the face of a policy or note to be paid at maturity.

Federal Deposit Insurance Corporation (FDIC): A federal agency that insures deposits up to $100,000 at commercial banks.

Federal Housing Administration: A U.S. government-sponsored agency that insures mortgages.

Federal Insurance Contributions Act (FICA): U.S. government legislation that mandates that employees contribute to the Social Security plan.

Federal Savings and Loan Insurance Corporation (FSLIC): A federal agency that insures deposits in savings and loans up to $100,000.

financial planner: A person who provides advice about identifying financial goals and strategies for meeting them.

fixed expenses: Expenses that you pay every week, month or year and over which you have little control, such as car payments and rent.

401(k): An employer-sponsored retirement plan.

fraud: Deception for personal gain by the means of false statements.

full-service broker: A stockbroker who provides services and information to clients in addition to facilitating trades.

gross annual income: Your total yearly receipts from your work, business and property before any deductions have been made for taxes or expenses.

growth fund: A mutual fund that invests in young companies that have the potential to grow very quickly. They usually pay low or no dividends, and the value of the stock has the potential to rise or fall quickly.

growth stock: A stock that has the potential of increasing its price as the company expands and prospers.

home equity loan: A loan that allows homeowners to borrow 70 to 80 percent of the appraised value of their house, minus what is owed on it.

illiquid: Describing an investment that is difficult to convert to cash.

income fund: A mutual fund that invests in older, well-established companies that grow slowly but steadily and pay relatively large dividends.

Individual Retirement Account: Employed persons can make annual contributions of up to $2,000 into this tax-deferred account. The owner of the account may make withdrawals from the account without penalty after the age of 59 1/2.

inflation: The rate at which the real cost of goods and services rises in the economy. The average rate of inflation, according to the U.S. Department of Labor, is about 5.4 percent. Because of inflation, a loaf of bread that costs $1 today would cost $2.86 in 20 years.

interest: Payment for money that is borrowed.

interest rate risk: The risk that rising interest rates will lower the market value of bonds issued earlier.

Internal Revenue Service (IRS): The U.S. federal agency that collects taxes and administers the tax laws.

investment: The money you put into some form of property for income or profit or into some form of security, such as a home or pension plan.

investment objectives: The goals that an investor sets for a portfolio.

investment return: The amount of value which your investment gains or loses over a given period of time. This is usually expressed as a percentage of the original amount invested. A 5-percent return means you earned $5 for every $100 you invested during that time period.

investor: Someone who gives money for the purpose of financial gain.

junk bond: A debt security graded less than BBB. Because it is rated so low by the bond rating companies, it produces a higher yield, but it is also a high-risk investment.

Keogh plan: A retirement plan for self-employed individuals.

laddered portfolio: When you build a laddered portfolio, you spread the dollar amount of your investment among securities with different maturity dates.

liability: An obligation to pay a certain amount to another party.

lien: A creditor's legal right to sell the mortgaged assets of a debtor when the debtor fails to meet loan payments.

limited payment life insurance: Whole life insurance paid for over a specified number of years.

liquid assets: Cash or savings easily converted into cash, such as stocks, bonds, and bank savings. Assets that are not liquid include real estate and collectibles.

market risk: The danger that the stock market as a whole will decline.

maturity: The time period of a loan.

maximum guaranteed premium: The most an insurance company is able to charge for coverage, as indicated by a contract.

money market account: Offered by banks, savings and loan institutions, and credit unions, these accounts are like checking accounts that pay interest. They are insured by the FDIC.

money market fund: A mutual fund that invests in short-term, low-risk nonequity securities such as commercial paper, Treasury bills, and certificates of deposit.

municipal bond: Debt security issued by cities that is free of federal taxes and may be exempt from state taxes if the purchaser lives in the state in which the issuing municipality is located.

mutual fund: An investment company that pools the resources of hundreds or thousands of individuals to enable them to diversify in a variety of investments, including stocks, bonds, and money markets.

net assets: The total assets minus the total liabilities of an individual or company.

net income: The money available to you after all taxes have been subtracted from your gross income.

New York Stock Exchange (NYSE): The largest and most active stock market in the world.

no-load fund: A mutual fund that does not charge a sales commission.

penny stock: An inexpensive stock usually issued for new business ventures. Because the underlying companies are unknown and possibly unstable, the potential for fraud is high.

pension plan: An arrangement that allows an employer to pay retirement benefits to employees.

Ponzi scheme: An investment fraud named after Charles A. Ponzi who ran a large scam of this type in the 1920s. It works on a pyramid principle whereby early investors are paid off with money coming from succeeding waves of investors, who lure more investors, the last of whom lose the most.

portfolio: A group of investments.

preferred stock: A type of stock that gives the stockholder first dibs over common stockholders to the assets and dividends of the company if the company goes out of business. Preferred stockholders are guaranteed fixed dividends but have no voting rights.

premium: A payment for an insurance policy.

principal: The orginal sum of money invested.

profit: Income that is left after expenses have been deducted.

profit-sharing plan: A plan offered by employers that allows employees to deposit a portion of the company's profits in a tax-deferred retirement account.

prospectus: A detailed brochure explaining the investment objectives, type of investments, management style, fees, risks and other information concerning a mutual fund or other investment.

pyramid scheme: [See: Ponzi scheme.]

rate of return: A measure of the income that an investment will yield.

real estate: Land and buildings.

revolving credit: A shopper can continue to incur more debt even as the old debt is being paid off. Usually there is a top limit to the amount of debt which can be incurred, based on the borrower's income.

rider: An endorsement that changes the terms of an existing insurance policy.

risk: The potential for the value or return on an investment to drop or be less than expected.

risk management: Determining how likely certain events will be, then taking steps to reduce any negative impact.

roll over: To reinvest funds from one account to another.

savings and loan: An institution that takes deposits and makes primarily real estate loans.

Securities and Exchange Commission (SEC): The federal regulatory agency that oversees the securities markets and administers the securities laws.

share: A single unit of ownership in a corporation or mutual fund.

shareholder: A person who owns stock in a corporation or mutual fund.

Social Security: The U.S. government-sponsored retirement plan.

speculation: The practice of purchasing stock based on its potential selling price instead of its actual value.

Standard & Poor's: A company that provides financial information including a stock index (S & P 500) and insurance ratings.

stock: A share of ownership in a corporation.

stock fund: A mutual fund that invests exclusively in equities.

stock market: A place where people buy and sell shares of corporate ownership.

stock market crash: An unusually large drop in the overall value of stock prices on a particular day.

stockbroker: A company that or an individual who facilitates a stock transaction but does not own the stock at the end of the sale.

straight life insurance: Whole life insurance with premiums payable until death.

tax bracket: A designation that determines what percentage of income must be paid in taxes. Theoretically, the more income an individual receives, the higher the tax bracket, and the larger the percentage of taxes will be due.

tax-deferred account: An account that contains funds that are not taxed until a later date.

tax shelter: An investment used for deferring, eliminating, or reducing income taxes.

10-K statement: A detailed analysis of a company's financial condition filed annually with the Securities and Exchange Commission.

term insurance: A policy payable at death if that event occurs during the specified term, or length, of the insurance.

unearned income: Income such as dividends, interest payments, or other income that is not received as a salary or wages.

universal life insurance: A type of insurance that enables the policyholder to purchase term insurance at a higher price and invest the difference in a tax-free account.

U.S. savings bond: A security issued by the U.S. Treasury, the interest of which is exempt from state and local taxes.

U.S. Treasury bill: A short-term debt security of the U.S. Treasury.

U.S. Treasury bond: A longer-term debt security of the U.S. Treasury.

U.S. Treasury note: Intermediate-term debt security of the U.S. Treasury.

variable income: Money you make sporadically, such as a bonus at work.

vested right: Your claim to a share of some future benefit, such as a pension, toward which you have paid or earned credits.

volatility: The price swings that an investment experiences over time.

whole life insurance: A term that refers to either straight life insurance on which premiums are payable until death, or limited payment life insurance, on which premiums are paid only for a certain number of years.

zero-coupon bond: A bond issued at a discount that increases in value as it approaches maturity, but provides no periodic interest payment.

RESOURCES

Books

The Beardstown Ladies' Common-Sense Investment Guide. The Beardstown
Ladies Investment Club with Leslie Whitaker (Hyperion, 1994).

*The Beardstown Ladies' Guide to Smart Spending for Big Savings: How to Save
for a Rainy Day Without Sacrificing Your Lifestyle.* Beardstown Ladies
Investment Club with Robin Dellabough (Hyperion, 1997).

Beating the Dow. Michael O'Higgins (HarperPerennial, 1992).

*The Best of Living Cheap News: Practical Advice on Saving Money and Living
Well.* Larry Roth (Contemporary Books, 1996).

The Budget Kit: The Common Cents Money Management Workbook, 2d edition.
Judy Lawrence (Dearborn Financial Publishing, 1997).

Ernst & Young's Personal Financial Planning Guide. Edited by Robert J.
Garner and Robert B. Coplan (John Wiley & Sons, 1996).

Money: 127 Answers to Your Most-Asked Financial Questions. Steven C. Camp
(November, 1995).

The Motley Fool Investment Guide. David Gardner and Tom Gardner (Simon
& Schuster, 1996).

1,001 Bright Ideas to Stretch Your Dollars: Pinch Your Pennies, Hoard Your Quarters, Collar Your Dollars. Cynthia G. Yates (Vine Books, 1995).

10 Minute Guide to Beating Debt. Susan Abentrod (MacMillan General Reference, 1996).

Magazines, Newspapers, and Other Publications

Barron's. 200 Liberty St., New York, NY 10281, (800) 568-7625, $145/yr., weekly.

BusinessWeek. 1221 Avenue of the Americas, New York, NY 10020, (800) 635-1200, $49.95/yr., weekly.

Consumer's Reports. P.O. Box 53029, Boulder, CO 80322, (800) 234-1645, $24/yr., monthly.

Forbes. 60 Fifth Ave., New York, NY 10011, (800) 888-9896, $57/yr., biweekly.

Fortune. P.O. Box 60001, Tampa, FL 33660, (800) 621-8000 $57/yr., biweekly.

Inc. P.O. Box 54129, Boulder, CO 80332, (800) 234-0999, $19/yr., 18 issues.

Investor's Business Daily. 12655 Beatrice St., Los Angeles, CA 90066, (800) 831-2525, $189.00/yr., daily.

Kiplinger's Personal Finance. 3401 East-West Highway, Hyattsville, MD 20782, (800) 544-0155, $19.95/yr., monthly.

Money. P.O. Box 60001, Tampa, FL 33660, (800) 633-9970, $39.95/yr. 13 issues.

The New York Times. P.O. Box 2047, S. Hackensack, NJ 07606,
(800) 631-2500, $374.40/yr., daily.

Smart Money. P.O. Box 7538, Red Oak, IA 51591,
(800) 444-4204, $15/yr., monthly.

The Wall Street Journal. 200 Liberty St., New York, NY 10011, (800) 568-
7625, $175.00 yr., daily.

Worth. P.O. Box 55420, Boulder, CO 80322, (800) 777-1851, $18.00/yr.,
ten issues.

Newsletters and Reports

Morningstar Mutual Funds. 225 W. Wacker Dr., Chicago, IL 60606, (800)
735-0700, $425/yr.

Standard & Poor's Stock Reports. 65 Broadway, New York, NY 10006, (800)
221-5277; (212) 770-4091. NYSE edition: $1,350.00/yr. weekly
updates or quarterly bound edition; AMEX and Nasdaq editions:
$1,080/yr., weekly updates or quarterly bound edition; CD-ROM edi-
tion: $1,095/yr., 24 updates.

The Value Line Investment Survey. P.O. Box 3988, New York, NY 10008,
(800) 833-0046, $570/yr., weekly.

Zacks Analyst Watch. Zacks Investment Research, 155 N. Wacker Dr.,
Chicago, IL 60606, (800) 399-6659, $295.00/yr., bimonthly.

Investment Clubs

National Association of Investors Corp. 711 W. Thirteen-Mile Road,
Madison Heights, MI 48071, (810) 583-6242. For listings of local
investment clubs in your area.

Organizations

American Consumer Credit Counseling. 24 Crescent St., Waltham, MA 01904, (617) 592-5700.

Consumers Union, 101 Truman Ave., Yonkers, NY 10703, (914) 378-2000.

Debt Counselors of America. P.O. Box 8587, Gaithersburg, MD 20898, (301) 762-5270; (800) 680-3328. Web site: http://www.dca.org

Duff & Phelps Credit Rating Company. 55 East Monroe St., Chicago, IL 60603, (312) 368-3157.

Fannie Mae (Federal National Mortgage Association). 3900 Wisconsin Ave. NW, Washington, DC 20016, (800) 7-FANNIE.

Federal Deposit Insurance Corporation (FDIC). Office of Consumer Programs, 550 17th Street NW, Washington, DC 20552, (202) 393-8400.

Moody's Investors Service. 99 Church St., New York, NY 10007, (212) 425-2606.

National Foundation for Consumer Credit Referral Line. 38505 Country Club Dr., Suite 210, Farmington Hills, MI 48331, (800) 388-2227.

National Fraud Information Center. P.O. 65868, Washington, DC 20035. (800) 876-7060. Web site: http://www.fraud.org

Securities and Exchange Commission. Office of Investor Education & Assistance, 450 Fifth St. NW, Washington, DC 202549, (202) 942-7040. Web site: http://www.sec.gov

Standard & Poor's Corporation. 25 Broadway, New York, NY 10007, (212) 425-2606.

INDEX